HOW TO
PARENT
WITH YOUR
EX

FOR THE NONRESIDENTIAL PARENT

Working Together
for Your Child's
Best Interest

BRETTE MCWHORTER
SEMBER
ATTORNEY AT LAW

SPHINX® PUBLISHING
AN IMPRINT OF SOURCEBOOKS, INC.®
NAPERVILLE, ILLINOIS

First Edition: 2005
Third Printing: April, 2006
Published by: **Sphinx® Publishing, An Imprint of Sourcebooks, Inc.®**

Naperville Office
P.O. Box 4410
Naperville, Illinois 60567-4410
630-961-3900
Fax: 630-961-2168
www.sourcebooks.com
www.SphinxLegal.com

This publication is designed to provide accurate and authoritative information in regard to the subject matter covered. It is sold with the understanding that the publisher is not engaged in rendering legal, accounting, or other professional service. If legal advice or other expert assistance is required, the services of a competent professional person should be sought.

From a Declaration of Principles Jointly Adopted by a Committee of the American Bar Association and a Committee of Publishers and Associations

This product is not a substitute for legal advice.

Disclaimer required by Texas statutes.

Library of Congress Cataloging-in-Publication Data
Sember, Brette McWhorter, 1968-
Parenting with your ex : working together for your child's best interest / by Brette McWhorter Sember.-- 1st ed.
    p. cm.
Bound in back-to-back format with separate sections for the residential and nonresidential parent.
Includes index.
ISBN 1-57248-479-9 (pbk. : alk. paper)
1. Parenting, Part-time. 2. Divorced parents. 3. Children of divorced parents. I. Title.
HQ755.8.S45 2005
649'.1'08653--dc22
                                                    2005006963

Printed and bound in the United States of America.

VP — 10 9 8 7 6 5 4 3

For Terry, Quinne, and Zayne

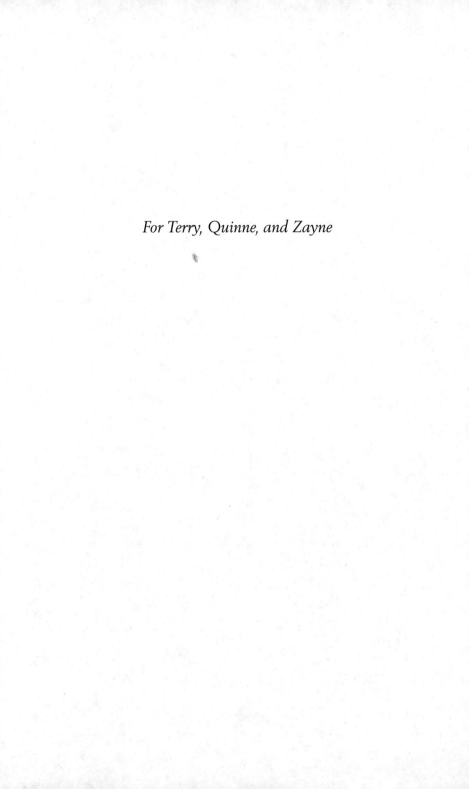

I would like to thank the children I worked with when I was practicing law, who led me to the deeply personal insights behind this book. Having worked so closely with them and having been so involved in their lives, I felt deeply compelled to write a book that would help their parents improve their situations. I offer my deepest respect and admiration for the judges and court personnel who handle these cases with such care and empathy.

Thanks also go out to my agent, Sheree Bykofsky, for her support and help; my parents, Thomas and Kathleen McWhorter, for everything they do; my friends and sounding boards, Belle Wong and Brigitte Thompson; Joanne Wilton, MSW, for discussing the initial concept of this book with me; my husband and children, who put up with my hours in front of a computer; and the dogs who warm my feet and heart as I write.

CONTENTS

PREFACE

This book is designed to be your complete guide to coping and living with a parenting plan. This book is two books in one—there is one side for each of the parents who have gone through a divorce or separation. In most divorces or separations, the child lives primarily with one parent (the residential parent) and spends time with the other parent (nonresidential parent). Both parents are equally important to the child.

This book has two separate parts in what is called a *flip book*. It is designed to fully address the unique concerns, situations, emotions, and difficulties faced by parents in each role. While the advice, examples, and problems described for each type of parent may be different, the underlying message is the same for each: focus on your child, learn to cope with dealing with the other parent, and move forward in your life as a parent.

The book is written in two parts, each with its own cover, chapters, and appendices, because both parents in a child's life are equally important and parents in each role face different problems and concerns. This book is a symbol of that.

Many books offer psychological perspectives on co-parenting, single parenthood, and life after divorce. This isn't one of those books. Written by a divorce and family attorney, this book gives you a practical road map for living with a parenting plan. The author worked in family court, representing both children and parents. She saw the problems families face as they try to navigate through post-divorce parenting and the changes it brings. This book is filled with practical tips that are based on her experience with real families.

There are lots of books that tell you how to get yourself and your child through the actual divorce, but none tell you how you are going to live in this new situation. It is difficult to adjust to a completely new life, and it is difficult to continue to manage parenting through the years following a divorce or separation. This book is your complete guide to dealing with parenting after divorce. Living with a post-divorce parenting plan is like nothing else you have done before. Many families have trouble coping with the challenges it brings. They end up returning to court, where they let the court work out their disputes and make changes to their schedule. Some families end up in a *revolving door* syndrome, where they are constantly returning to court on a regular basis. This constant uncertainty takes its toll on the parents—and especially on the child.

This book will help you avoid the revolving door. It is a guide for you to use now, and for you to return to again and again as your child grows, your situation changes, and new challenges and obstacles arise.

It is important to note that both males and females take on both of the parenting roles discussed in this book. If you are a non-residential mother or a residential father, you might sometimes feel like you are in an unusual role. This book helps all divorced parents, regardless of their gender and regardless of which role they are in.

This book is also unique in that it is written for parents in both the United States and Canada. The problems concerning living with a parenting plan are universal, and are not specific to certain states or countries. Each half of the book contains an extensive appendix that will help you find resources, support groups, books, and websites that can help you. A separate appendix has been created with Canadian resources for Canadian parents.

The book carefully refers to "the other parent" throughout the text. This is a purposeful attempt to get you to think of him or her in this way. He or she is your child's other parent, and it is important for your child's health and well-being that you respect and accept this fact. Try to avoid thinking of him or her as your ex, former spouse, and so on. Keep your focus on your joint parenting responsibilities.

This wording is also used because many parents never marry each other. It is common for people to become a couple, have a child, and then separate. This book is written for you whether you have been married or not, are divorced or separated, are currently in the midst of divorcing or separating, or even if you and the other parent never even had any long-term relationship at all, but did have a child together.

The book generally refers to "your child." Obviously, many people have more than one child. If you have more than one child, apply the advice given to all of your children. When the text refers to your child, this generally includes children and teens of all ages. If a situation is different for teens, it will be specifically mentioned. The book will help you understand the different reactions children will have at different ages and also discusses how sibling relationships are affected by visitation.

Both parents are needed in a child's life. You should be commended for wanting to focus on your child's needs. This book will help you through the difficulties visitation brings, and will help you and your child make the most of your situation.

This unique flip book is written for both you and the other parent. After you have read the side written for you, you might want to read the side that is written for the other parent, so that you can look at things from his or her perspective. Share this book with the other parent.

Refer to this book when you are first adjusting to living with a parenting plan and in the future. Problems and concerns that you cannot anticipate are certain to come up at a later time. Keep this book as a reference guide to use for those situations down the road.

NOTE

If your relationship with the other parent was abusive or if you feel that you could be in danger because of the other parent, this book is not designed for you. If you feel you are in danger, you should speak to your attorney or get help from a shelter for battered spouses. If you feel your child is in danger from the other parent, you should contact your attorney and your local department of family and children's services.

INTRODUCTION

You have faced the end of your marriage or relationship, been through the courts or mediation, and now your child is living primarily with the other parent and spending time with you. You may not consider your custody and visitation arrangement to be ideal but it's the plan you're all going to have to live with. Now that you are through the craziness of the legal process and the difficult emotions that accompany it, your first order of business has to be taking everything that has happened in your life, in court and inside you, and just letting it settle in. You will have to work through it all somehow for your own sanity.

There are many books and resources available to help you heal the pain of divorce. This is not one of them. This book is designed to help you manage, understand, and maximize your parenting time. The book is written not by a psychologist or social worker, but by an attorney who has spent much time in court and in the homes of families facing and working through parenting plans. The author worked one-on-one with parents and children, many of them on a daily basis, as they struggled though the unraveling and reformation of their families. Some families were able to make their new situation work for them, but many more could not. These were the families who returned to court again and again as one or both of the parents continued to have problems living with the new arrangement.

Many families get caught in a revolving door, returning every few months to court to try once again to get something changed, when what really needs to change is their behavior and attitudes. This book offers practical, to-the-point solutions for the problems that you as a nonresidential parent are facing or about to face. If you can follow the advice in this book, you can avoid the family court revolving door syndrome and you can maximize your parenting time—improving life for you and your child. Whether you share joint custody or the other parent has residential custody, you are still both parents and your child will benefit if you can learn to co-parent together effectively.

The book is designed to help you through the confusing, upsetting, and sometimes hurtful process of being the nonresidential parent. No matter what has led you to this point, you are your child's parent, and the role you play in his or her life is incredibly important. Your child has two parents and needs to be part of both of your lives. The time you spend with your child is very important. You are important to your child and are not any less of a parent simply because your child spends a bit more time with the other parent.

You may feel constrained by the schedule you have to follow. You may find that it isn't completely convenient for you, and you probably feel that it doesn't give you enough time with your child. Despite all of that, you are responsible for making the most of the time you do have. Your child will not judge you by the times you aren't there, but by the times you are. This book contains pointers and tips to help you make the most of what you have. It is based on the author's experiences working with families that have gone through the same process you are now going through.

This book will discuss what you can expect from your child, yourself, and the other parent, as well as other people in your life and your child's life with regard to the parenting schedule. The book focuses on how to manage your parenting time as a practical matter, how to cope with it on an emotional level, how to help your child cope with it, and how to use it to benefit both of you. Each chapter deals with specific problems that come up during visitation and the different problems that come with children of different ages.

The advice is based on the author's firsthand, up close experiences as a divorce and family attorney and mediator. The author's years of experience working as a Law Guardian for children who are the subjects of custody and visitation cases brings the unique perspective of one who has watched the divorce process through the eyes of those children.

Many parents walk out of the courthouse with an order naming them as the nonresidential parent, and feel that they have somehow lost or that the other parent has somehow won. You must get all these thoughts out of your head. You have to accept that whatever the judge decided or you agreed to is now how you will live your life. You must focus on making your time with your child the best it can be and helping your child adjust to it. This book will help you do just that.

You have an important and essential role in your child's life and the words of a court order don't change or impact that. Your mission must be to make the most of the time you have with your child.

How to Use This Book

Read this book and pay careful attention to the chapters that speak to your immediate concerns or problems. Keep the book handy and consult it as you experience new problems and different stages.

The book is designed to be your guidebook as you live with a parenting plan and all of the complications and problems it can create. Many parents resolve their custody cases through settlement or a trial, head out to live with their parenting plan, and end up back in the courtroom within a year because of practical problems with visitation. These problems can stem from any of the parties— the residential parent, you, or even the child. Problems can include things such as a child not wanting to go on visitation, a residential parent who tries to limit or interfere with visitation, and even disagreements over things like the child's laundry or homework.

Divorce completely rearranges the lives of everyone involved. An adjustment period is necessary. Many families do not make it through the adjustment period without having to seek legal intervention. This book will help you with that difficult period and will steer you away from the pitfalls that bring so many families back through the courtroom door.

What this Book Cannot Do

What this book cannot do is change the facts of your situation. If you are certain that the parenting plan you have is not in the best interest of your child or is completely incompatible with your schedule, you need to contact an attorney or deal with the issue in mediation. Should you ever become concerned that your child is being physically or mentally abused, you need to take immediate action and contact your local police department or child protection agency. This book cannot change the other parent. But this book can help you learn to work with him or her.

Your parenting plan or custody and visitation order is nothing more than a schedule that organizes everyone's time. It is not a decree that you are a bad or unimportant parent and that the other parent is the better parent or has more clout with regard to the child. It is merely a time management tool. Learning how to make the most of what you have will help your child be healthy and feel loved, and will bring you sanity. You can make visitation a wonderful part of your child's life as well as your own life. Making the best of this situation is the best thing you will ever do for your child.

1

MOVING FORWARD

Now that the dust from the divorce has cleared and you know what kind of parenting arrangement you are going to have to live with, it is time to face reality. First, you need to completely understand what your parenting plan is and what rights you have. Next, you will need to take a look at what that really means for you and your child. While it may be hard to adjust to your new life, you will find that there are many bright spots in it. This chapter will help you get a grip on your life and help you see what you have to smile about.

Legal Terms

Now that you have visitation, you might not be entirely sure what rights that gives you. First you need to read the judge's order or your settlement agreement carefully. The following are some of the possible custody and visitation arrangements you might have.

Joint Custody with Visitation. You and the other parent share joint custody, with the child residing with the other parent and spending time with you. Joint custody means the parents are supposed to make decisions together about the child, such as where he or she goes to school, whether to have medical procedures done, etc. Joint custodians are expected to be able to communicate with each other. The person the child lives with has *residential custody*. The other parent sees the child according to the parenting schedule or when agreed upon.

Sole Custody and Visitation. In this arrangement, the other parent has sole custody and you have visitation. This means the child lives primarily with the other parent and that parent makes most of the decisions about the child and is not required to get your input. You have visitation at set times or at times as agreed upon.

Shared Custody. In this scenario, the child splits his or her time equally between the parents. Both you and the other parent are responsible for making decisions about the child. Neither parent is considered to be the residential parent.

If you are not sure which type of arrangement you have, call your attorney or mediator for help in understanding the wording in your judgment or order.

Being Flexible

When you are awarded visitation, you are given the right to see your child at the times outlined in your order. What many parents do not realize is that you are not limited to this. You and the other parent can agree to arrange visitation at other times, change the times that are scheduled by the court, and basically make any adjustments you want. However, you must both agree to it. You must be certain that you can either trust the other parent to stick to the changes you agree to or you need to get it in writing so that you have proof of the agreement in case there is ever a problem. It is true that a court order is a legal, binding document. However, almost all custody or divorce decrees add that in addition to the scheduled visitation times, the parents shall have time with the child *as agreed upon.* This gives you the freedom to change the schedule as you need.

Judges want parents to take control of their schedule and adjust it to suit their family's needs. They do not want families returning to court to change pick-up times or arrange for a change to the holiday schedule. The court hopes you will become self-sufficient and learn to work together to make changes.

Visitation is not something that is set in stone, and should be something that changes as you, the other parent, and the child change. What works for a one-year-old will not work when the child is in kindergarten or in high school. You and the other parent should view visitation as a guideline, not as a hard and set law. (See Chapter 6 for more about communicating with the other parent.)

Dealing with Labels

You should not get hung up on the words *custody* and *visitation*. You also should not become too focused on the word *co-parenting*. These are simply terms used to describe the situation that exists after divorce. Many parents feel they have been branded as a bad parent if they do not get joint or shared custody. This is not the case at all. Your arrangement might have been what the judge believed was best or simplest, or maybe he or she didn't even care and just picked a schedule. However it happened, this is the situation and no one is going to benefit if you let the words get to you. Remember *sticks and stones may break my bones, but names will never hurt me?* Those are words you are going to have to come to live by if you are going to help your child and yourself through what lies ahead.

The most important thing to remember about the different arrangements is that they are just words. Your child is still your child. No one can take that away. Learn what arrangement you have and then *forget it*. Children are not something you get *custody* of. The only time people are taken into custody is when they are arrested. There is nothing remotely militant about being a parent. Your focus should be on your relationship with your child, not on a phrase and how it makes you feel or how other people react to it. The reality is that you are your child's parent and nothing else matters.

You also should not get hung up on the word *visitation*. It sounds downright insulting that the court or the other parent expects you to *visit* with your own child. In fact, many attorneys, mediators, and judges are moving away from this poor choice of words and are now talking about *parenting time, parenting access, parenting plans,* and *parenting schedules.* Use these words if they make you feel more comfortable. Try to see past the words to what is at the heart of the matter—your child. When you are with

3

your child, you are living together. Parents and children share lives, not a schedule.

You must decide that you are not going to feel intimidated or lessened by the fact that you are the nonresidential parent. You aren't any less of a parent because of the living arrangements. It can be hard to deal with this label, particularly if the other parent acts as if he or she has *won* or been anointed head parenting god. The important thing to remember is that you have a crucial role in your child's life.

Adjusting to Your New Situation

Now that you have digested the legal terms and gotten past them, you need to face another big mental challenge—nothing in your life will ever be the same. That statement may seem to be huge, unfair, and unbearable, but it is true. Your relationship with the other parent did not work and you have parted. You are living apart, and this means that in order for your child to receive the benefit of being loved and supported by both parents, all of you must make changes and concessions to adapt to this new way of life.

Just because a situation is different does not mean it can't be as good—or better—than the previous situation. Think about how unhappy everyone was when the relationship was coming apart. It was not a healthy situation for your child or for anyone else. You got out because you knew this was true. You now have the chance to build your own life and make your own way. In order to include your child in this, you will have to make arrangements to do so. This means that you will have to make concessions. Things may not be ideal, but you have to get past it and focus on what is good in your life. One of the best things in your life is your child.

The months or years you spent as a nuclear family have ended. You cannot get them back and that is okay. Your job now is to look to the future and find a way to keep parenting as a central priority in your life. There are good times ahead for you and your child. You are still a family.

The divorce was difficult for everyone, but now your child has the chance to spend time with two parents who love him or her and who are living independent, happy lives. You are a wonderful role model for your child. You're living a life that hopefully allows you to find fulfillment and happiness. You can be yourself and give your child the best you have to offer.

Dealing with Anger

You and the other parent broke up because you fought, were unhappy, or blamed each other for things. Thankfully, that scenario is over. You do not need to live with anger on a daily basis now. Certainly you are going to continue to feel some anger and you probably have many things to blame the other parent for—but it does not need to be a central part of your life now.

If you continue to focus on anger and blame (no matter how well justified it may be), you are never going to be able to get past it and find happiness on your own. There is no way you can always be angry without having it affect your child. As difficult as the divorce or separation has been for you, it has been at least a hundred times more difficult for your child.

Everything that has happened has been magnified through your child's eyes, increased by total or partial incomprehension and heavily laced with emotional insecurity and fear. When you are angry around your child, he or she unconsciously interprets some or all of that anger as being directed towards him or her. Think about this—every time you are angry, your child assumes it is because of him or her. Your anger has a very strong effect.

To build a successful independent relationship with your child, you have to be able to focus mentally and emotionally. Anger is going to get in the way. You need some space in your head and your heart to make a plan for how you are going to parent from now on. If you are angry, you are using a lot of energy and effort for your anger.

Remind yourself that the other parent is *not* worth all the effort and angst. Decide that you are not going to waste your energy on him or her.

Now, none of this means that you are not going to experience anger in the future. It is most assured that you and the other parent will continue to push each other's buttons. The two of you had a lot of practice and it is a habit. You're going to have to steer through these situations in the months ahead. If you haul along baggage from the past it is just going to be harder to manage.

You are also experiencing a lot of hurt and loss. Some things have happened that you did not deserve. You may have been rejected or insulted or you may be upset about the way the parenting plan worked out. Take the time to grieve for what you have lost, to feel the pain that is associated with a relationship ending, and then face the future. You may never completely get over what has happened. In a way, the pain will always be a part of you, but you have to move forward now. Resolve to make a fresh start. You aren't perfect and, of course, you're going to slip up—but try very hard to focus on your relationship with your child and not on your failed relationship with the other parent. You have a lot of work ahead, but you are going to get through this successfully.

Be Positive

You might have sought residential custody and lost. You may have been awarded the amount of visitation you wanted or you may have gotten less. Whatever you were given is now a reality, and you have to find a way to assimilate it into your life and into your child's life. The best approach is to be positive. Don't focus on the time you have lost with your child or the unfairness of the situation. Instead, think about the wonderful stretches of time that are now just for the two of you. There need not be any bickering or negotiating over when you can have parenting time. You have it by court order, and now all you have to do is relax a bit and let it become a part of your life. There is no point in agonizing over what you wanted, how unfair the system is, or how wrong the judge was. This will not help you or your child. Take what you do have and get the most that you can out of it.

You can now parent your child on your own without interference from the other parent. That may come as a big relief. You may also realize you now have some time to yourself. Instead of using this time to feel sad or angry because you are not with your child, try to enjoy it by doing fun things and rediscovering who you are.

Make Your Child Your Priority

You need to focus on your relationship with your child. But how exactly are you going to go about this? The first step you have to take is to realize that even though your relationship with the other parent ended, you are and will always be an essential part of your child's family. Visitation should not be viewed by you as an obligation, but as an opportunity.

You need to remember and reassure yourself that your role as a parent is important, makes a difference, and is essential. Think about a time when your child needed you desperately—maybe she fell off her bike and needed you to bandage her knee, or maybe his turtle died and he needed your love and reassurance. Think of how nothing else in the world mattered at that moment except what your child needed and the way you could ease the pain. Now think about how your child must be feeling right now. He or she might be very confused, sad, angry, or depressed. Picture these feelings as a big scrape—like one from falling off a bike—except it is inside and you can't see it. Now think of how you would care for a cut knee— with gentleness, patience, a bit of reality, sympathy, and love. Your child needs a big dose of this medicine and you are the only one who can provide it. Think of this wound your child has and set out to help it heal.

Push aside everything that is going on in your life (within reason) and focus on your child when he or she is with you. Let him or her know that you are always going to be available, that you can never stop being a parent, and that your love will never change.

Write your parenting time in big letters on your calendar and let nothing get in the way. Especially when you are just beginning the adjustment process, you need to block time out of your life and give it to your child.

> **WAYS TO MOVE FORWARD AS A NONRESIDENTIAL PARENT**
> ➤ Focus on the time you have together, not the time you will be apart.
> ➤ Do not let your child see or hear the anger or resentment you feel towards the other parent.
> ➤ Give visitation priority in your life.
> ➤ Show respect for your child's relationship with the other parent.
> ➤ Think about how your child is feeling and how you can help.
> ➤ Do not allow your expectations to be too high for your time together.
> ➤ Make room in your home for your child.
> ➤ Have contact with your child when you are not together, by phone, email, etc.
> ➤ Be patient with your child and with yourself.
> ➤ Remember that your time with your child belongs to you and your child—the other parent is not in charge of it or involved in it.
> ➤ Use the time when your child is not with you to fill your own needs and interests.
> ➤ Stop feeling guilty that you can't be with your child as much as you would like.
> ➤ Position yourself as an involved and important person in your child's life.

Focusing on your child also means that you need to reevaluate your entire situation. When you see the other parent, you may see red. You should turn your eyes to your child and make him or her the focus of the situation. Make time to call your child when you won't have time with him or her for a few days. But you can't think about your child all the time, and you shouldn't. You have a life to live, and your child will benefit if you are a well-rounded person with a job, activities, and friends. It can be easy though to turn off that part of yourself that is a parent because it is too painful to cope with when you don't see your child every day. No matter how often you see your child, you are a parent all the time. No one can change the important role you play in your child's life. You're a permanent part of his or her life, and always will be. Make room in your life, your schedule, and in your home for your child. When you fail to make time for your child, you are not punishing yourself or the other parent. You are punishing your child.

As you first experience being a nonresidential parent, it will be difficult to juggle all the changes you are facing. It will get easier and you will find a new routine that incorporates parenting time into your normal life. Your child will come to adjust to it as well, and you will have a new, comfortable family unit. There are plenty of good times ahead!

2

UNDERSTANDING YOUR RELATIONSHIP WITH YOUR CHILD

If you haven't realized it yet, your relationship with your child changes as a result of the divorce or separation. Your child probably grew up with two parents involved in all decisions. You and the other parent made decisions together, or at least, you were both involved in some way. Now your child is parented by two parents who are in separate homes and who no longer act as a team. Your child has gone from getting essentially an average of the two of you to getting the two extremes. This is a huge change for everyone.

Your child is dealing with one or possibly two new residences, as well as a schedule that could be very confusing and hard to adjust to. All of these changes have had an effect on your child and may cause him or her to act differently. You are learning to be single and to adjust to having scheduled time with your child. You will find that this will cause you to act differently.

You have also gone through some rough times. You have gone through the breakup of a relationship, a court proceeding, and all the deep emotional difficulties these two very stressful situations have brought. You're probably not who you used to be. You can see that both you and your child have changed, so it makes sense that your relationship has changed and will continue to change.

Reactions to Divorce

A great deal of research has been conducted to study the effects of divorce on children. While these studies reveal some basic truths, the fact is that each child is unique and may react individually. Read about some of the common effects, but keep in mind that your child may not be typical.

CHILDREN'S COMMON REACTIONS TO DIVORCE

- ➤ Sadness and grief
- ➤ Anger
- ➤ Desire to place blame (on parents and on themselves)
- ➤ Fear of abandonment
- ➤ Divided loyalties (wanting to be loyal to both parents, even when this is impossible)
- ➤ Denial
- ➤ School and social problems
- ➤ Withdrawal
- ➤ Inability to trust people or form bonds
- ➤ Low self-esteem
- ➤ Physical symptoms such as stomachaches and headaches

Ages and Stages

Expect preschool children to blame themselves and possibly to regress or go backwards a bit in their development. School-age children experience worries about the future and are at a higher risk of depression. These children also often *act out*.

Teenagers frequently take sides in a divorce and experience financial worries because of it. They also reflect negatively on marriage as an institution and try to physically and emotionally distance themselves from home and home life. (See Chapter 12 for more information about how reactions differ by age and how to deal with them.)

Girls and Boys

Girls are likely to react by trying to make connections with males or by trying to bring male influences into the female parent's home. Girls in general try to be perfect to prevent future problems. Boys are likely to react by trying to fill their father's shoes by acting as the man of the house. When at their mother's home, boys try to suppress their feelings of great sadness and may become more aggressive. Low self-esteem can be a problem for both. (For more information about children's reactions, refer to the resources listed in Appendices B and C.)

Getting through Hard Times

Just as you cannot have good times all the time, you won't have bad times that never end. You may have some very difficult periods of time to get through, but they will pass. The beauty of children is that they are always growing and changing.

If you find that there truly are no happy times, you need to evaluate your situation. Are you the one who is perceiving everything as unhappy? If so, you might want to talk to a mental health professional. Depression can be treated. You have been through a lot and there is nothing wrong with finding someone who can help you deal with what you have experienced. If your child is the one who sees everything negatively, give the situation some thought. Is there something you are doing to add a negative edge to everything? Can you encourage your child to lighten up a bit? If nothing seems to help, your child might be suffering from depression. You need to find a mental health professional who is experienced in working with children and get some outside help. Discuss this with the other parent. You also might consider seeing a counselor with your child to help sort out what is happening and how you can improve things.

SYMPTOMS OF DEPRESSION IN CHILDREN

➤ Persistent sad or irritable mood
➤ Loss of interest in activities once enjoyed
➤ Significant change in appetite or body weight
➤ Difficulty sleeping or oversleeping
➤ Psychomotor agitation or retardation
➤ Loss of energy
➤ Feelings of worthlessness or inappropriate guilt
➤ Difficulty concentrating
➤ Recurrent thoughts of death or suicide
➤ Frequent vague, non-specific physical complaints, such as headaches, muscle aches, stomachaches, or tiredness
➤ Frequent absences from school or poor performance in school
➤ Talk of or efforts to run away from home
➤ Outbursts of shouting, complaining, unexplained irritability, or crying
➤ Being bored
➤ Lack of interest in playing with friends
➤ Alcohol or substance abuse
➤ Social isolation
➤ Poor communication
➤ Fear of death
➤ Extreme sensitivity to rejection or failure
➤ Increased irritability, anger, or hostility
➤ Reckless behavior
➤ Difficulty with relationships

(The National Institute of Mental Health, National Institute of Health Publication No. 00-4744)

If your child has four or more symptoms, it is a good idea to see a therapist, counselor, or doctor.

For the most part, you can expect there to be an end to unhappy times. You might find that there are some changes you can make to your life, to the visitation schedule, or to the way in which you deal with the other parent that can make huge improvements in the way you and your child view the world. It could be as simple as altering the time that visitation starts or ends, or agreeing not to discuss schedule changes in front of your child. Later chapters discuss these possibilities in greater detail.

Every nonresidential parent experiences ups and downs with his or her children. There were probably ups and downs when you were all living together as a family, so you shouldn't be surprised to experience them now. Focus on the good days and know that as everyone adjusts there will be more good days than bad days.

Dealing with Your Child's Anger

Both you and your child probably feel some sort of anger or resentment towards each other and towards the other parent. This is normal. All families experience this at times. When you first discover that your child is angry with you, it may come as a great shock. It really is a normal part of the adjustment process.

The Introduction and Chapter 1 discussed how to deal with and get past your own feelings, now it is the time to talk about how to help your child cope with his or hers. Many children will be frightened by their own feelings and unable to understand or verbalize what they are really experiencing. You are not a therapist—you are a parent. No one expects you to be able to handle these feelings perfectly. Of course it hurts you to think your child is angry. Of course, it just makes you even angrier at the other parent and at yourself. Of course it makes you sick to think that your child may blame himself or herself for the divorce, separation, or visitation scenario. You might also feel angry with your child about the way he or she is treating you. Your reaction is normal and so is your child's.

The first thing you must do, even if you are a person who does not often talk about feelings, is to tell your child flat out that absolutely none of this is his or her fault and that nothing could have been done to change any of it. Children do not automatically know this. They need to be told. You will need to tell your child this on many occasions before it will really sink in. You need to tell your child that you love him or her very much and that nothing will ever change that. Reassure your child that you will always be a part of his or her life, and that being available is important to you. You should tell your child that it is perfectly fine for him or her to be angry at you, at the other parent, and at the world if necessary. Say that you want your child to tell you about anything that bothers him or her. You need to really listen to what your child says. Try not to categorize or define the feelings for him or her, and let them come out and accept them without judgment.

Anger is a normal reaction to divorce, so expect that your child will experience it, either now or in the future. Try to remember that much of the anger is directed at the situation and not really at you.

Talk to Your Child

You need to open up a little bit about yourself. Tell your child that you are sorry too that there was a divorce or end of relationship and that it has been hard for you too. You need to talk about your *feelings* only. Your child needs to know that you have experienced hurt, sadness, and anger, but your child also needs to know that you are going to move forward and that you will always have lots of time and space in your life for him or her. You should not dwell on what you are going through. You are talking to your child, not a friend or confidant.

Emphasize that what happened with the other parent only had to do with your marriage or relationship. You are all still a family, but in a different way.

As the parent who does not live with your child full-time, you might encounter some anger that is specifically directed at you because of the living arrangements. Some children become angry and feel that the nonresidential parent didn't want them or didn't try hard enough to get custody. Your child might say that if you really cared, you would not have moved out or left.

Even if you feel it's all the other parent's fault that you became the nonresidential parent, do not tell your child that. Say that you and the other parent did what you thought would work best, or that the judge made a decision about what he or she thought was best for the family. It's not a perfect arrangement, but you have time together and that's what matters.

While all of the above might sounds pretty simplistic and more appropriate for younger children, teens need to get this same message from you. Your teen may not be willing to really discuss these things, but they are things that you need to say.

Do not expect this talk to be a cure-all. Instead, see it as a beginning. Keep the lines of communication open and try to find a way to talk about problems and feelings instead of yelling about them or closing up. It takes a lot of time to work through these things, and there is no quick fix.

There may be a time when your child or teen says something such as, "I hate you," or "I wish you weren't my mom/dad." These are difficult words to hear, but they are fairly common. Do not panic, flip out, or blow your top. Of course, hearing your child say something like this hurts, but remember that your child does not truly mean it. In the heat of the moment it sounds pretty believable, but you have to remember that your child is, in fact, just a child.

You cannot expect him or her to have a mature reaction or take the time to really process his or her feelings in a complicated way. The best way to handle this is either to not react at all or to calmly say, "I'm sorry you feel that way." Do not try to get into a lengthy discussion or try to convince your child he or she is wrong. This really will pass. It is a temporary and very common reaction.

Your child may also say something at some point indicating that he or she blames you entirely for the divorce or separation. Preteens and teens sometimes reach a point where they decide they have the entire situation figured out and can assign blame to one parent. This is a tough period to work through. You have to remain calm, even though inside you are furious that your child thinks this. You can tell your child that a divorce or separation is never one person's fault and there are many reasons that only the people who were in the situation could ever truly understand. Don't get into all the reasons why you believe the other parent is at fault.

Dealing with Your Child's Fears

Your child has lost his or her nuclear family. One or both parents have moved to new residences. You and the other parent have decided you don't want to live together anymore. Your child may naturally fear that you and the other parent may decide you don't love him or her next. Even teens may have this kind of subconscious fear. Everything in your child's universe has been substantially altered. Think for a moment how terrifying that is.

You need to let your child know that you are not abandoning him or her. You and the other parent have decided to change some things about where and how you live, and it has nothing to do with the child. He or she has a home at both places now and there will *always* be a place for him or her.

Neither parent can ever decide not to love the child. Explain that there is a difference in the way moms and dads love each other and the way they love their kids. Moms and dads choose each other and decide to live together. They can decide not to live together. Parents and kids do not choose each other and cannot decide they don't want to be together anymore.

Loving a spouse is like wearing a hat. You can take it off if you want to, if you have to, or if it gets uncomfortable. Loving a child is like having a head. You can never take it off, get rid of it, or truly change it. It is a part of you always. If your child is a teen, this explanation is too basic. You do need to state that people in a marriage can change how they feel, but that parents cannot. Remember that your child does not know what it feels like to feel a parent's love for a child. Explain how it makes you feel and how it is a part of you that can never change.

It is also important to explain that you never wanted to have to live apart from your child. The marriage or relationship ended and your child had to have one home. You did not want to leave him or her. Either the judge or the situation dictated that this is how it had to be. *Do not* blame the other parent for this. Explain that you would have the child with you all the time if you could, but that wouldn't be fair to the other parent. You are going to share time so that you both will be an important part of his or her life.

Give your child a card with all of your phone numbers so he or she can always reach you. Preschool and elementary age children may be frightened or worried if they don't know where you are. This gives the child the ability to contact you at any time and helps bring home the fact that whether you are at work or at your new home, that the child can reach you whenever he or she needs to. Take your child to see your new home and drive the child past your place of work so that he or she can have a visual picture of where you are. This way, you haven't disappeared—you are simply in another place. Show your child a photo of him or her that you keep on your desk, on your refrigerator, or in your wallet and explain that you are always thinking of him or her with at least one part of your brain. If your child is a teen, be accessible by email as well as phone. Let him or her know you are available when he or she needs you.

You should also expect that when your child is with you, he or she may feel abandoned by the other parent. You make sure the child can call the other parent whenever needed to ease this feeling. Reassure your child that the other parent misses him or her as well, and that they will be together soon.

Helping your child through these feelings is a long process, but with time and consistency you will notice an improvement.

Conflicting Loyalties

Children of divorce often feel pulled in two directions. They want to take both parents' sides. When with one parent, they say bad things about the other. They want to please whoever they are with. Children end up feeling confused and angry. The best way to cope with divided loyalties is to acknowledge they are going to happen and not encourage them. Never discuss your unpleasant feelings or opinions about the other parent with the child. Do not try to get your child to see your side of the story. Do not try to convince the child that you are right and the other parent is wrong.

There should not be any sides as far as your children are concerned. Your child has two parents who love him or her, but who disagree about some things. The disagreements are not something the child needs to be involved in or concerned with. If your child expresses opinions about the other parent, be available to listen, but do not become involved with the conflict by intervening, agreeing with the child, or criticizing the other parent. Talk to the other parent about this and see if you can both agree not to do these things. If the other parent does try to play on the divided

19

loyalties, you should not do so in retaliation. Stand your ground. (Read more about this in Chapter 4.)

Your Emotional Changes

You need to realize that you are going to experience changes in the way you feel as your new life as a nonresidential parent plays out. There are going to be days when you feel you will simply die if you can't see your child. Get through these days by going on one moment at a time. Look forward to the next time you will be together or think about good times you have had in the past. Distract yourself with work, friends, or family. Alcohol (or drugs) will not distract you and will only make the entire situation worse and endanger your relationship with your child.

There will also be days where you are happy to find yourself with the freedom to go anywhere and do anything without parenting obligations. You are not a bad parent for enjoying some freedom—you do not need to feel guilty. It's important that you come to enjoy all the good things about your new life.

You will find that your feelings towards your child may change. Some days you will feel like you know everything about your child, and other days he or she may be like a stranger who has a whole other life that you are excluded from. When you feel very connected and comfortable, let your child know. Give hugs, say how happy you are feeling, or just enjoy it. If you feel excluded, ask questions and make conversation so you can feel included. Never, ever accuse your child of leaving you out or cutting you off. You want to convey positive or constructive feelings whenever possible. If your child really is trying to cut you out, calmly explain that you'd like to be involved in his or her life or activities. Discuss it without putting blame on the child. Remember, these are normal reactions.

All of your feelings are real and important, but they are not all appropriate to share with your child. Confide in a friend or relative, but keep your child off your emotional roller coaster.

There will be times when you are angry with your child. This doesn't make you a bad parent. Before the marriage or relationship ended, there were times when you became angry with your child. It is normal to have this happen occasionally. Be certain that you control your anger, but feel free to be human and express it reasonably.

Your Child's Emotional Changes

Just as you are on an emotional roller coaster, so is your child. One day he or she wants to be with you every second and the next day he or she refuses to get into your car, or "forgets" about visitation. Your best bet is to not react in the heat of the moment. Count to ten if you have to before reacting. Be loving and supportive and look at the big picture.

This does not mean that anything your child does can be excused because of the trauma of divorce. There are standards of behavior that your child must meet and you as a parent are the one to set them and enforce them. You can give some leeway when needed, but you cannot allow a child's emotions to control you or your life. (Chapter 4 deals with this in-depth.) Just keep in mind that all of these extreme moods can't and don't last forever. Stick to your schedule and do not give in.

Many experts compare the divorce (or separation) adjustment process with the grieving process. Understand that your child has many stages and phases to go through—just as you do—in order to accept what has happened. You also need to know that often children have delayed reactions to divorce. They may not scream and shout when you tell them about the divorce the first time. It may take months for their emotions to fully develop about the situation. As children grow older, they begin to process the divorce or separation differently and may have different reactions with each passing year. Be patient.

If you find that you need help dealing with your child's emotions, there are many things you can do.

♦ *Talk to the other parent if possible.* Compare notes and see if you can hit upon a solution together.
♦ *Talk to a counselor.* You can see a counselor and get some ideas for how to cope without having to involve your child in counseling or you can have your child meet with a counselor.
♦ *Talk to your child's teacher.* Teachers can often offer insights about a child's behavior.

Remember that children's emotions are not always clear and they are not easily categorized. Talk about what is in front of you, but realize there may be more to it that you are hearing about. Learn to ask non-critical, open-ended questions that will help draw your child out and bring a wide range of emotions to the forefront. Don't be afraid to get help from counselors or therapists.

Learn to roll with the punches when it comes to dealing with emotions during visitation. If your child is being clingy, you may want to change your plans to take him or her to a get-together with your friends. If he or she is determined to be angry with you, you might want to get out of the house and do something to take both your minds off the situation, or you might decide to just let him or her spend the afternoon listening to music. Be prepared to be flexible. Remember that you have feelings as well, and there are times when they are going to clash with your child's feelings.

Good Times and Bad Times

One of the most important things to expect about the adjustment you and your child are making is that there will be ups and downs. You may have a terrific weekend together and feel as if you are getting back on track, and then you may have a few bad weeks. Remember that adjusting to the situation is a lengthy process. Nothing that happens is going to be set in stone. Good times and bad times are to be expected. Everything is going to be in flux for quite a while.

When you are experiencing good times, enjoy them. Let yourself relax and be happy. You might be able to pick your child up for visitation without a fight with the other parent or your child might be thrilled to see you. You might spend some time just playing together at your house and find yourselves being comfortable and feeling really connected. If you have a day like this, enjoy it.

Do not expect it to last and do not be disappointed when something happens to bring the good times to an end. If your child has a tantrum and says, "I hate you," if you become tired of playing Barbies, or your time together has to come to an end, don't see it as the end of the world. All children have short attention spans, all children and teens have tantrums, and no parent is perfect. Don't expect perfection from yourself or your child and you won't be disappointed. You must also remember that as a parent, it is not your job to make sure your child is happy every moment and has everything he or she wants. It is your job to make and enforce rules, give and receive love openly, and be willing to communicate. You are not a playmate or someone whose job it is to please your child. (Read Chapter 4 for more about establishing rules.)

Try to see everything that happens as part of the big picture. One bad day does not seem so terrible in the context of a month or a year. Keep your perspective.

You also need to understand that even as you and your child become accustomed to the new arrangements, changes will happen in your lives that can send things up into the air again. You might have to move to a different city, or your child may enter high school or join a sports team. You and your child are always changing, and so your situation will constantly be changing as well.

You aren't going to handle all of this perfectly and no one expects you to. Be yourself and try to put parenting first on your list of priorities. You and your child will adjust.

3

TALKING WITH YOUR CHILD

Once you no longer see your child on a daily basis, it can become harder to feel as if you communicate well with each other. While you are adjusting to the new schedule, you need to pay careful attention to how you are communicating with your child. Eventually, things will become easier and you won't need to constantly monitor what you say or how you say it.

You are going through a difficult time and it may be hard to control your emotions in a time with so much turmoil. However, you need to for the sake of your child. It may seem too much to expect that you have to put your child first when you probably feel as if nobody has put you first in a long time. There may also be times in the years ahead when it seems as though communication with your child is breaking down. But, it will be worth it to work through these problems. If you can take a few months and pay attention to your communications with your child, you will find that you can rebuild any bonds you might have thought were lost or damaged. Come back to this chapter then and review the suggestions.

Communication Do's

Of course you know how to talk to your child, but it can be helpful to have some things firmly in your mind that you need to communicate.

♦ *Say the unsaid.* After a divorce, you need to verbalize things that you normally would not need to say. You probably normally wouldn't need to tell your child "I could never hate you" or "You will always have two parents." But after divorce, your child needs to hear these things.

♦ *Remember to praise.* Tell your child when he or she succeeds at something. Remind your child that he or she is good at certain things.

♦ *Talk about the divorce.* Discuss the divorce without getting angry about the other parent. You can't pretend it didn't happen.

♦ *Be sincere.* Don't say what you think you should, say what you mean and what is important to you. You have to be yourself, no matter what.

♦ *Be honest.* This does not mean being harsh, overly detailed, or very negative, even when talking about the divorce. But you shouldn't sugarcoat things.

♦ *Focus on the present.* Talk to your child about his or her life and activities. Be involved in his or her day to day life and recognize it is important. You can't change what has happened, but you can help your child know that you are still and will always be involved in his or her life. Being a part of the small parts of your child's life will mean a lot to him or her.

♦ *Be positive about the other parent.* Emphasize the good in the other parent, even if you aren't really sold on it yourself. Be happy when he or she has a good time with the other parent, not resentful.

THINGS TO SAY TO YOUR CHILD

➤ I love you.

➤ You are always going to be part of my family.

➤ I am happy to be with you.

➤ I am so proud of the way you _____.

➤ I know this is difficult for you.

➤ I am always willing to listen to anything you need to talk about.

➤ This is your home as well.

➤ Your mother/father and I disagree about some things, and that's okay.

➤ Mom/Dad and I divorced each other, but not you. We will always be your parents and we will work hard to parent together.

➤ One of the reasons we got divorced was because we disagreed about too many things. You and I can disagree and you don't have to worry that we will ever lose each other.

➤ Moms and dads can get divorced, but parents and kids never can.

➤ Your Mom/Dad will always be your Mom/Dad and that's how I want it.

➤ This is the schedule we are going to be using. I'd like to know how you feel about it.

➤ Your friends are welcome to visit here at our house.

➤ When we are not together, I think about you and am happy to know I will be seeing you again soon.

➤ You can call Mom/Dad anytime you want to from here.

➤ How did your presentation go at school today?

➤ Where did you and your friend ride to on your bikes yesterday?

➤ Why don't you ask Mom/Dad to help you with that. He/She is good at things like that.

➤ What would you like to do tonight?

continued...

> We are not going to get back together. I know that would make you happy, but the divorce is final and neither one of us wants to get back together.

> Where do you think we should go on our vacation together?

> We are using this schedule because we think it is the best way to share our time with you. We both would be with you all the time if we could, but we can't.

> It isn't anyone's fault that we got divorced. Sometimes marriages just don't work out.

> I moved out because the fighting wasn't good for any of us.

> How great that Mom/Dad took you to the zoo. What did you see there?

> I wish I could be with you all the time, too, but then you would never see mom/dad. It's important that we share time with you.

> This is your home too. You have two homes and it's important to me that you feel like this is a place where you live.

Communication Don'ts

You aren't perfect, so there are going to be things that fly out of your mouth sometimes without thinking. It's okay to be human and you can't beat yourself up about it. But you can try to keep in mind the kinds of conversations and comments that will not be very helpful to your child.

♦ *Do not say bad things about the other parent.* Think how hurt you would be if someone criticized someone you love. That's how your child feels when you say bad things about the other parent. It is okay to let your child know that you and the other parent have differences, but it is not okay to insult, demean, or degrade the other parent. You know what he or she has done wrong, but keep it to yourself.

♦ *Do not suggest that your child must choose between you.* Children want to please both parents and can often end up in a tailspin trying to make them both happy.

♦ *Do not share your personal details.* You must keep the adult details of the divorce, your turmoil, and your emotions to yourself. Your child is not a friend or a shoulder to lean on. Adult information is only for adults. Don't talk about your loneliness, your heartache, your anger, or your sadness. Use friends and family for those topics.

♦ *Do not talk about money.* Don't get your child involved in your financial problems. It's okay to explain you can't afford something, but it is not okay to detail what exactly you got in the divorce and how you can't afford the child support payments.

♦ *Do not ask your child to spy or carry messages.* Your child is not a go between and should never be asked to tell the other parent something or even deliver a note. The child is subject to the other parent's emotional reaction and will feel as if the anger is meant for him or her. Your child is not a spy who can keep you up to date on the other parent's life and should not be asked to bring back reports.

♦ *Do not make promises you can't keep.* It is easy to sometimes say things out of wishful thinking, but your child needs promises he or she can rely on.

♦ *Do not pry for details.* It is good to talk with your child about what he or she did with the other parent. It is an important part of his or her life and it shouldn't be something that is taboo to discuss. But don't start prying for details or get too involved in finding out exactly what happened. The information you get is not going to be very accurate anyhow since children's perceptions are skewed by their own self-interest.

THINGS NOT TO SAY TO YOUR CHILD

➤ Your mother/father is dishonest/mean/stupid/cruel/lazy/cheap, etc.

➤ You are going to have to choose which parent you want to be with.

➤ You always side with your mother/father.

➤ You are just like your mother/father.

➤ Ever since the divorce, I have felt so alone.

➤ When you leave I am all alone.

➤ Don't you wish you could see me more?

➤ Sometimes I just want to kill myself.

➤ I pay your mother/father a lot of money so you will have new clothes and he/she just spends it on other things.

➤ If he/she doesn't think it is enough, he/she can just take me to court for more money.

➤ Do you know how much you are costing me each month?

➤ We can't go to the movies because your mother/father took all the money from me in the divorce.

➤ Who was that man/woman at the house when I picked you up?

➤ Tell your mother/father that I am not paying another dime this month.

➤ Where is Mom/Dad going tonight?

➤ Don't tell Mom/Dad we did this.

➤ Which one of us do you love more?

➤ I want you to know this is all your mother's/father's fault.

➤ Tell Mom/Dad that I can't pick you up until 7 next Friday.

➤ Give your mother/father this check and say that it's all I have right now.

➤ You should tell Mom/Dad that you love me more.

➤ Watch out for men/women. They take what they want and throw you aside.

➤ Don't ever get married. You'll regret it.

continued...

> ➤ I hardly ever get to see you.
> ➤ You don't even miss me.
> ➤ You probably don't even think about me when you're not here.
> ➤ This is the only time I get to see you and you're ignoring me!
> ➤ Why don't you call Mom/Dad and ask if you can stay a little longer?
> ➤ I'm going to win back custody of you someday.
> ➤ If you lived with me, you would be able to stay up later/ buy more clothes/have parties/get a new computer/ have a puppy.

Developing Your Listening Skills

To truly communicate with your child, you need to listen to what he or she is telling you—verbally and nonverbally. Pay attention to his or her reactions to things and draw conclusions.

Ask open-ended questions to get him or her to open up. Show interest in the things he or she is doing and thinking. Listen to what he or she is talking about and respond.

Expect children under age 8 to ask repeated questions about the divorce, the schedule, the other parent, etc. Answer these questions even if you feel as if you already did. The repetition will show your child that this new world he or she is living in is dependable.

Your child may, at some point, tell you that he or she would rather live with you. Usually this happens when there is some problem with the other parent, but it is also common from an older child of the same sex. Find out what the problem or situation is first. Don't go running to your lawyer to seek a change of custody. There are cases where a change of custody is needed, but in most cases, this is your child's way of letting you know how important you are to him or her, or pointing out a problem at the other home.

If your older child is serious about this, then you need to discuss this with the other parent. Making a change in residence is a big step for everyone and should only happen when it is something that is best for the child.

4

SETTING GUIDELINES FOR YOUR CHILD

The most important thing for a child who has experienced a divorce or separation is normalcy. Children need to feel that, although their parents' relationship has drastically changed, many things in their own lives will remain stable. It is crucial now more than ever that your child feels there are things in life that he or she can count on.

One of the best ways to help a child feel rooted, protected, and loved is to have rules. Think about what life was like when you and the other parent lived together. You had a set of rules your child was expected to follow. In most families, these rules are unspoken, but everyone understands what they are. Children usually have some chores they are responsible for; there are set times for things such as meals, baths, and homework; and, there is behavior and speech that is not acceptable.

Now that you and the other parent have divorced or separated, it is important that your child continue to have rules and responsibilities. Life goes on, and maintaining rules and continuing to expect certain things from your child will demonstrate this to your child. It is important that your child understands that even though you will not be together all the time, there will still be rules when he or she is with you.

Some parents feel as if they should give their child a break. After all, he or she has been through a lot and expecting him or her to take out the garbage or clean the hamster cage seems like an extra burden. Continuing to live normal lives where everyone has responsibilities and jobs is the best way to help your child get on track with the new situation. Life isn't carefree and easy, and it is silly to pretend that it can be. Of course, it is fine to make exceptions to the rules, but you have got to have the rules or your everyday life will just fall apart. Rules actually make things easier for kids, because they provide them with set boundaries and limits. Knowing what is expected and how to behave can make children feel comfortable and eliminate confusion.

Some nonresidential parents feel so desperate to get positive feedback from their kids that they use all their time with their child for fun, special treats. It might seem like your child enjoys these, but you're not connecting on a real, everyday basis. The fun is going to wear thin unless you develop a normal life together. To do this you must have rules and expectations for your child.

Rules for Two Homes

In an ideal world, the rules that were in place before the divorce or separation are the rules that you should continue to use. This will give your child a sense of continuity and will also lessen the potential for disagreement with the child and with the other parent.

In reality, most parents find that they need to make changes to house rules after a divorce or separation. Schedules change, as do the children's emotional needs, and nothing can ever be as it was. Many parents who have left the family home and gone on to create their own home feel they should be able to create the rules that will be followed in their own homes. If you feel this way, you are right to a certain extent. It is your home, and you can decide how you will live and what rules you will follow. Taking responsibility for your own rules is an important part of coping with divorce. However, it is important to remember that your child now has two homes to live in and two parents to obey separately. It is just simpler if the rules in both homes are the same or very similar—particularly if your child is very young. This also lets your child know that you and the other parent will continue to parent together and that there is still a family unit that has importance in the child's life.

Rule-Making with the Other Parent

Arrange to speak to the other parent sometime when your child is not around and say you would like to discuss the rules that your child will be following in both homes. Explain that you believe it makes sense for both of you to have rules for your child that are the same or similar, and you would like to work together to create rules that will work in both homes. By doing so, you are *not* asking the other parent to get involved in your life or to tell you what to do. You are, however, suggesting that the two of you cooperate to make life better for your child.

RULES TO DISCUSS WITH THE OTHER PARENT

➤ Bedtime

➤ Waking up time

➤ How often bathing should occur

➤ When homework should be done

➤ Household chores (There will be differences between the households, but the main point is that there should be some at each home, and the time and difficulty levels should be similar.)

➤ Unacceptable behavior, language, and attitudes

➤ Unacceptable foods or limits on certain foods (For example, some doctors recommend limiting daily juice intake in babies, toddlers, and preschoolers, and soda intake for all children. Some children have food allergies, while others have religious restrictions on diet.)

➤ School attendance

➤ When medication must be taken

➤ The standard by which the child must keep his or her room clean

➤ Church and religious class attendance

continued...

> ➤ When friends may come over and when the child may visit friends
> ➤ Curfew
> ➤ Amount of television time
> ➤ Amount of telephone time
> ➤ Amount of computer/video game time
> ➤ Teeth brushing, flossing, and other hygiene
> ➤ Naps (for younger children)
> ➤ Anything else either of you feels is important

The goal is to try to keep most of the rules the same at both homes, but you and the other parent will probably find that some rules need adjustments. It is also important to remember that you may not agree about all of these rules. In that case, you will need to compromise—you could decide one rule and the other parent could decide another, or else you could reach a decision on a rule that is halfway between the two opinions (an 8:30 bedtime if one person says 8 and one says 9). You may also realize that some rules need to be different in each home. If this is what you both agree will work best, then it's fine. If you are unable to agree or compromise, then you will each have to set your own rules.

You will gradually reach a point where you don't need to discuss certain rules. You are not going to spend the rest of your lives negotiating a list of rules with each other. Eventually, things will evolve to the point where most things are understood and don't require long discussions. As your child grows up and reaches new milestones (getting his or her driver's license, getting a job, beginning to date, joining a sports team, and so on), it will be helpful to talk with the other parent about rules again.

Ways to Talk about Rules with Your Child
If most of the rules will remain the same, it probably won't be necessary for you to have a formal conversation with your child about them. Just make the rules a part of your daily life when the child is at your home. If something will be changing, discuss it with your child.

Some parents find that it is useful to post the house rules at each home, especially if you have a child who has trouble handling rules or if the rules at the two homes are very different.

SAMPLE HOUSE RULES LIST

1. We do not yell at each other or hit each other.
2. We always treat each other with respect and kindness.
3. Bedtime is at 9:00 p.m. on school nights and 9:30 p.m. on other nights.
4. Dirty laundry is to be placed in the hamper.
5. Everyone must clear his or her own dishes off the table.
6. Jahleesa is responsible for folding all of the laundry.
7. Every Tuesday night the hamster cage will be cleaned out by Jamal.
8. Homework must be done before TV or computer time.
9. If you spill it, you clean it up.
10. All beds must be made before breakfast.
11. We will take turns loading the dishwasher.
12. Whoever is home on Saturday morning will help clean the house.
13. Phone calls are limited to no more than 20 minutes.

Some younger children benefit from a sticker chart, where the child gets a sticker placed on the chart for each chore that is done or every rule that is followed that day. If a sticker is awarded in every category for an entire day or an entire week, a special reward, such as a video or a small toy, can help reinforce positive behavior.

SAMPLE STICKER CHART

Cara's Sticker Chart	Mon.	Tues.	Wed.	Thurs.	Fri.	Sat.	Sun.
Put away her toys							
Did not throw anything							
Brushed her teeth							
Played nicely with dog							
Carried her dishes to the sink							
Washed her hands before eating							
Placed her shoes beside her bed							
Was quiet while adults were talking							

Some parents of teens like to have a contract with their child. The contract contains all of the rules the teen must follow and consequences for breaking those rules. Both parents and the child sign it and agree to follow it. Sometimes these contracts also list what responsibilities the parents are committing to (listening to the child without judgment, attending the child's sporting or extracurricular events, and providing transportation to outings with friends, etc.).

SAMPLE CONTRACT WITH A TEEN

Chase White and his father Tom White enter into this contract and agree to follow it for the next four months.

1. The parties agree that they will not swear or shout.
2. On the days Chase is home, he will take out the trash, make his bed, and help do the dishes.
3. Chase will do his homework before he goes out with friends or watches TV.
4. Chase will set his alarm and make sure he is on time for school.
5. Chase will be home by 11 p.m. on weekends when he is home. If he is late, he will be grounded the next weekend day he is here.
6. Chase will not ride in a car with an unlicensed driver.
7. Chase will not have female guests over when Tom is not home.
8. Chase will earn $20 for every grade higher than a B on his report card.
9. Tom will not work on Sundays when Chase is home and will spend the day with him instead.

| Chase Williams | date | Thomas Williams | date |

| | | Mary Williams | date |

Independent Rule-Making

Because you now live on your own, in a separate place and your lifestyle has changed, there will be situations that arise at your home that were never an issue when you all lived together as a family. For example, perhaps you now live near a bus stop. You will need to formulate rules as to whether your child can ride the bus alone, where he or she may go and who will pay the fare.

You don't need to initiate a discussion about these decisions with the other parent, since they happen at your house only, unless you would like to get some input. Realize though that the other parent may hear about these new things and wish to discuss them with you. Don't view this as an attempt by the other parent to question your authority or undermine you. Briefly and calmly give a simple explanation. Remember, you both should be involved in your child's life, but the other parent cannot dictate what the rules will be at your home.

The flip side to this is that things have changed for the other parent as well, and he or she may find it necessary to formulate some new rules that pertain to new situations happening at that home. You may hear about things that concern you from your child. Calmly ask the other parent about these new situations and rules so that you can be informed. Remember that you have no authority to dictate what the rules will be in the other home, but you do have the right to understand them so you can know what your child is doing and so you can support the rules. It is also important that you do not question the basis for these rules in front of your child.

As a parent, your job is help your child obey and live with rules no matter who has created them and whether they are right or wrong. You would not suggest to your child that his or her teacher is wrong and that a rule at school should not be obeyed because you don't agree with it. You need to respect the other parent's rules in the same way.

When You Disagree with the Other Parent

You and the other parent clearly have different opinions about some things—that's why you are no longer together. Occasions will arise where you feel the other parent has made a rule that is wrong. The best way to handle this is to discuss it with him or her when your child is not present.

Step back and evaluate just how important it is. If the other parent has a rule that your child must vacuum his or her room twice a week and you feel that is excessive, take a look at the situation. Is this rule going to do serious harm to your child? Just because a child is unhappy about a rule does not mean it is wrong.

If the other parent has a rule that the child may cross a busy street alone and you believe the child is too young and could be harmed, then you do need to make an effort to get the other parent to change the rule by having a calm and reasonable discussion about it. (See Chapter 6 for more information about communicating with the other parent.) If you feel rules persist at the other home that are dangerous to your child or completely unreasonable, you need to speak to your attorney to get outside help as discussed in Chapter 13.

Things Your Child Reports

When dealing with the other parent's rules, you have to remember that what your child tells you may not be entirely correct or complete. Before you fly off the handle, get the information from the other parent. Things usually aren't as bad as they sound, and even if a rule seems wrong on its face, an explanation from the other parent may show why it was necessary.

Making Exceptions

When you lived together as a family, there were times when the rules were bent, or on occasion, completely thrown out the window. A special family gathering may have resulted in a late bedtime, a busy week may have meant household chores were skipped, and so on. Just because you are trying to provide continuity and stability does not mean you are a prison guard. It is perfectly fine to bend the rules and make exceptions, as long as you don't do it all the time. Flexibility is an important part of parenting. However, you should not fall into a trap where you create rules and then allow them to be broken in order to win your child's favor. Use exceptions judiciously.

Remaining Flexible

As children get older, many things in their lives change—amount of homework, curfew, eating habits, sleep needs, time with friends, etc. Rules for some of these things just gradually change with the child. Other times, you need to formally change a rule. If your child is 8 years old and has a 8:30 p.m. bedtime, soon he or she will be older and able to stay up later.

When you notice that a rule needs to be changed, try to discuss it with the other parent. He or she has probably noticed the same thing and both of you have probably begun to make adjustments. As your child gets older and as the trauma of the divorce or separation gets farther into the past, your child will be more comfortable with the notion of two homes, and having some rules that are different at each home will no longer be as difficult to handle. Additionally, older children can handle two sets of rules easier than younger children. You will eventually reach a point where things are run one way at your home and another way at the other parent's home, and it is not a problem for anyone.

Consequences

Part of having rules is having consequences when they are broken. When you and the other parent meet to discuss what the basic rules will be, you need to discuss what the appropriate types of repercussions are for broken rules. Some parents find it helpful to write these down. You need to agree that you won't question the other parent's use of these consequences and will not interfere with them.

It is important to discuss whether punishments will apply at both homes. For example, if your teen breaks curfew at your home and is grounded by you for three days, will this be three consecutive days and apply at whichever home the child is at, or will it only apply to the next three days the child is at your home? Expecting the other parent to enforce your punishments is not easy for anyone. You need to decide together how to handle these situations.

It is important to note that mental health experts generally discourage the use of physical punishment. Physical punishment is never a good idea, and can be especially dangerous when you have a former spouse on the look out for child abuse. Protect yourself and your child and avoid physical punishment.

Coping with Rules

When you and your child are first adjusting to life after divorce, there will be conflict about rules, and the child will find many opportunities to tell you that you are being unfair or that your rules are not the same as the other parent's. Also, as your child grows older, he or she may complain that some rules are now unfair. This is normal. It is part of adjusting and part of growing up. Your job is to hold steady and don't give in (other than once in a while), unless you truly believe a rule needs to be changed. Make sure you take the time to talk to your child about rules and consider his or her input. Eventually, you will find that you get into a routine where every rule is no longer questioned. Don't give up just because things get rocky. Your child will love and respect you more if you have consistent and fair rules that are evenly applied, even if he or she squawks in the short term.

Keep in mind that in order for your child to grow up believing that he or she is still part of a family, and that he or she has two parents who love and believe in him or her, you need to demonstrate respect and consideration for the other parent. Even if you believe he or she has random rules and ineffective punishments, don't tell your child. Be a model for your child by showing him or her that it is important to treat other people with respect and consideration (despite their behaviors), and that rules must be followed no matter how random or wrong they seem. Encourage your child to voice his or her opinion about rules, but remind him or her that parents make the rules. You and the other parent are still parenting together, and in order to do so, you must support each other's decisions, rules, and consequences.

5

SETTING EXPECTATIONS FOR YOURSELF

In order for your parenting plan to work, you need to consciously make an effort to make it work. Being divorced or separated and living on your own does not mean things are going to be free and easy for you. Things are going to be difficult for a while until you, your child, and the other parent have adjusted to your new lives. To get through the difficult adjustment period and create a plan for the future, you need to have some basic rules or a plan for yourself to follow. There will also be times in the future when things will become difficult. Return to this chapter then to help you cope.

Managing Emotions

You have a lot to cope with in terms of your feelings of loss, anger, frustration, depression, love, grief, and fear. Allow yourself to recognize what you are feeling and deal with your emotions. Suppressing and denying your feelings is not the answer—you need to face them and work through them. However, you do have to find a way to control your emotions around your child and the other parent. You and your child need to focus on maintaining your relationship—not on rehashing the divorce. Your feelings about the divorce or separation are for *you* to deal with. Your child has an enormous amount of emotion to handle him- or herself without trying to understand yours. Try to control your emotions the best you can.

You and the other parent are no longer emotional partners, and you need to separate yourself from him or her emotionally, while continuing to parent together. Try to work together whenever possible. It's not always easy to do this and there are sure to be some frustrating points along the way, but you can get through it and work together for your child.

Watch Your Words

Your child still has another parent and spends most of his or her time with that parent. You cannot pretend that the other parent doesn't exist, or that part of your child's life doesn't exist or isn't important. Your child will talk about the other parent because he or she is an important part of the child's life. You should not try to stop your child from discussing the other parent. You want your child to talk to you about the important things in his or her life, and the other parent is one of those things.

While you want your child to talk freely about the other parent, you do need to monitor what comes out of your own mouth about the other parent in front of your child. Resolve to never say anything derogatory, insulting, cruel or negative about the other parent. That does not mean you cannot think it, just don't say it. Your child loves the other parent and will always have a relationship with him or her. You must allow this and you must not try to get your child to see the other parent's "true colors." You must let your child have a separate relationship with the other parent, and allow him or her to draw his or her own conclusions.

Just as you must bite your tongue sometimes when speaking to the other parent (see Chapter 6 for guidelines on this), there are times when you need to bite your tongue around your child. Do not let negative comments about the other parent slip out. Never negatively compare your child to the other parent. (Do not say, for example, "you're as thoughtless as your mother.") Avoid arguments and nonproductive discussions with the other parent, especially in front of your child. Try to be as civil as possible to the other parent. It won't always be easy, but it will help your child. (See Chapter 6 for more about this.)

As a parent, it is your job to support your child's relationship with the other parent, not to undermine it.

Talk to Your Child

Having open lines of communication with your child is essential, but don't talk all about you—what you are doing, what you are feeling, etc. Of course, you must share some of your thoughts and feelings in order to have a good relationship with your child, but it should not be all about you.

Avoid talking about everything that went wrong in the relationship with the other parent or your longing for the past. That being said, you cannot act as though the past never happened. It is normal and healthy to mention something that sparks a memory you share. ("That's just like the time we all went camping and Mom got lost in the woods.") You have a shared past and it is unhealthy to pretend it did not happen.

Try to avoid being overly critical of your child while you are all adjusting to your new lives or to a recent change in the situation. You are bound to be more irritable, more easily hurt and more easily annoyed during this period. You have to find a way to bite some of it back.

There will probably be a time when your child complains to you about the other parent. Listen to what the child has to say, but do not become involved in the dispute. A good answer is to tell the child that you are glad he or she feels comfortable telling you about this, but that it is something he or she needs to discuss with the other parent. The exception to this is if your child is in danger or is extremely upset. (See Chapter 13 for information about how to intervene.)

How to Talk about the Divorce or Separation

There will be times when your child will ask you questions about why you divorced and how you feel about the other parent. It is important to be honest, yet not negative. Instead of saying, "Your mother is a selfish *#%! and I couldn't put up with it anymore," or "Your father was sleeping around," you should give an answer like, "Mom and I disagreed about a lot of things," or "Dad and I decided that we wanted to live our lives differently." It's important to make it clear that neither parent is at fault and also that you will not be getting back together (since most children harbor hope for this).

Making Promises

Do not make promises you can't keep. Period. Do not promise your child you will see him or her every weekend if you won't be able to. Do not promise to call if you cannot. Do not say things just to make your child feel better at the moment, and then forget or neglect to follow up on them.

It is much better to be honest with your child. If your child wants to see you every weekend, instead of promising that you will, explain why you can't—but do express how you feel about this. Say you miss him or her, too, and that you are sad when you are apart, but that you try to focus on how happy it will be the next time you are together.

Make promises that are realistic. If you do have to break a promise, be honest about it and tell your child right away. Explain what has happened and why you can't keep your promise. Everyone breaks promises once in a while, but you don't want to get in the habit of doing this all the time.

There will be times when things will come up and you will need to change the schedule. Changing the schedule is different than not showing up. If something comes up, reschedule. Arrange things with the other parent and if possible, let your child know what has happened.

Be There

When you are supposed to spend time with your child, be there. Do not skip visitation. If you can't come, call and let your child and the other parent know. Some parents avoid telling their child they have to miss a scheduled visitation. Think of how he or she will feel if you just don't show up. Yes, he or she will be disappointed when you say you won't be coming, but that is not as disappointing as being stood up by a parent. And when you are there, really *be there*. Give your child your undivided attention. Turn off your cell phone and give your child

100%. It really is not the amount of time you share with your child that matters, but what you make of the time you have.

Be On Time

It is important that you set up parenting times at times when you are available. Waiting at the window for your car to arrive for 45 minutes will upset your child and send a message that you do not care. Your child already has some feelings of abandonment. Don't make them worse. When you have made a commitment to be with your child, be on time. It is also important to be on time when you are returning your child home. Doing these things will demonstrate to your child that your time together is important, and also demonstrate to the other parent that you are honoring the schedule and are responsible and respectful of him or her (and if you do this, it's a good first step towards reciprocal action from the other parent). Of course, you have nothing to prove to the other parent, but this will make it easier for you to negotiate changes or ask for favors in the future.

Some nonresidential parents believe that being late, not showing up, or screwing with the schedule is a good way to stick it to the other parent. The only person you're hurting when you do this is your child.

Promise yourself that you will be on time. If you are going to be late for an unforeseen reason, call and let your child and the other parent know. If you find that you are regularly late, you need to make some schedule changes so that you can regularly get there on time.

Paying Child Support

Whether you feel it is fair or not, child support is the law. The court has determined what you are obligated to pay. It is difficult to turn over large sums of money to the other parent. You must get past this. Think of it as a promise you have made to your child and honor it. Of course, the value and importance of your parenting and relationship cannot be evaluated in a dollar amount (many parents feel as if they are paying for the privilege of visitation). Money should have nothing to do with it. Also, many nonresidential parents are angered when they see that the other parent does

49

not use this money directly for the child's benefit. However, by following the law and meeting your obligations, you show your child that you are a good example and that you care enough about him or her to meet your obligations. If you don't pay it, you will likely have to return to court. Inevitably, your child will find out why and will likely feel hurt on some level.

Additionally, it is important to understand that child support and parenting time are not interconnected. Some parents mistakenly think that if they have their child with them for a week, they don't need to pay child support that week. Child support is a separate issue and is not tied to how much time you spend with your child.

Additionally, the other parent cannot stop you from seeing your child if you are behind on child support payments. If this happens, talk to your lawyer.

Make the Most of the Time You Have

Being a nonresidential parent is nobody's dream. But the fact of the matter is, this is your role. You must find a way to live with it and make it work for you. You must promise yourself from the outset that you will make the most of the time you have with your child. This is different from setting unreasonably high expectations for yourself. It's not going to be perfect and it's not going to come easily.

Your time with your child will not always be idyllic, cozy, and wonderful. This doesn't mean that you shouldn't give it all you've got. Don't be discouraged if things are not perfect. Give your child your full attention whenever possible, be emotionally available for your child, and always look for the bright side. If you approach an afternoon with your child by thinking, "Four hours is just not enough and there is no way we can connect in that time frame," then it's likely your prediction will come true. But if you face the time with a positive outlook and are glad to have time with your child, then the time will be as good as it can be—not perfect, but still good.

Continue to have a life. Your job, friends, and family are important to you, and you need to continue to give them time and importance in your life. When you are active, happy, and fulfilled, you are a better parent. Build a new life for yourself and include your child in it.

RULES TO SET FOR YOURSELF

➤ Do not confide in your child about all of your feelings about the divorce.

➤ Make time for your child in your life. Visitation must be a priority.

➤ Be on time in all your dealings with your child.

➤ Be honest with your child about the fact that reconciliation is not going to happen.

➤ Find a way to cope with your emotions. See a therapist or talk with friends.

➤ Live your own life. Maintain your job, your friendships, and your family relationships. To be a good parent, you must have your own life.

➤ Never speak negatively about the other parent in front of your child.

➤ Do not have expectations that are too high.

➤ Show your love for your child.

➤ Resolve to cope with your emotions and move on with your life.

➤ Find pleasure in life and share it with your child.

➤ Don't make promises to your child that you cannot keep.

➤ See yourself as emotionally separate from the other parent.

➤ Avoid confrontations with the other parent. (See Chapter 6 for more information about communicating with the other parent.)

➤ Expect things to be difficult for a while.

➤ Stop blaming yourself and focus on the positive things in your life.

➤ Make your home a place in which you are comfortable.

➤ Pay your child support.

➤ See visitation as an opportunity, not an obligation.

6

DEALING WITH
THE OTHER PARENT

It is likely that one of the reasons you and the other parent are no longer together is because you have difficulty communicating and understanding each other. You probably both harbor some negative feelings. Despite all of this, you are going to have to develop some way to talk to each other and exchange information so you and your child can receive the benefits of visitation. Even if you have a detailed, court-ordered visitation plan, problems and conflicts are going to arise that will require communication. Finding a way to communicate will certainly not be easy, but will make parenting together easier. If it is easier, you may be able to arrange it more often! If things are easier, everyone certainly will experience less stress.

Create a New Partnership
You and the other parent are going to be parents together for the rest of your lives. Even though you are divorced or not together anymore, the parenting part of your relationship continues. Try to sit down and talk to each other simply as parents, not as two people whose marriage or relationship went bad. If you can both agree that you each want what is best for your child, then you can find a way to achieve it together. Resolve to be co-parents. Agree not to argue about past events and to talk only about the foreseeable future. It

takes a lot of work and effort to develop a new parenting relationship with each other, but it is worth it.

It is easy to fall back into your old patterns of arguing, disagreeing, and trying to hurt each other. Agree that you will not let this happen. Think about how important your child is to you. You cannot change who your child's other parent is, no matter how much you might want to. You can only focus on finding a way to cooperate with him or her to make life better for your child.

These are promises that are not easy to keep. You are both human, and will both slip up. Accept that you will both break the rules once in a while, but try to overlook the mistakes and focus on keeping your child's happiness your priority. Remind yourself constantly that you are doing this for your child.

You both know you have to parent together, but if you can actually verbalize this to each other it can go a long way toward making you really committed to it. Tell the other parent that your goal is to respect him or her and help your child continue to have a meaningful relationship with him or her. There may be all kinds of bad feelings between you and the other parent, but if you can just tell him or her that you will try to work together, you will most likely have offered an olive branch that will help you parent together effectively.

Develop Guidelines

If you and the other parent are going to make your parenting plan go smoothly, you need to set up some basic rules you will both follow. The following are some examples of rules that will help both of you cope. Read these rules and then develop your own rules that apply to your situation.

- ♦ Schedule changes must be requested as soon as possible and preferably no later than 24 hours in advance.
- ♦ You each will try your best to accommodate schedule changes requested by the other parent.
- ♦ If the parent picking up or dropping off the child is going to be more than 15 minutes late, he or she will call.

- Decide if you will enter each other's homes at pick up/drop off or wait in the car or outside. You have to decide how comfortable you both are with these situations.
- Decide who will be responsible for washing the clothes taken to the nonresidential parents home. You may be surprised to learn that this is often one of the most common problems that arises in dealing with visitation!
- Any items taken with your child will be returned with the child (especially crucial items—blankie, jacket, sneakers, school books, instrument, sports uniforms, favorite toy).
- Agree to work together to create rules for your child.
- Agree not to argue in front of your child. Whenever an argument starts, develop a word or phrase you will both recognize that will indicate that this is something you should discuss later, out of earshot of your child (such as *later*, or *table it*).
- Your child is not permitted to make changes in the schedule without permission from both of you.
- You will not use your child to transmit messages or money to each other.
- You will contact each other directly, either in person, by phone, by email, or in writing.
- You will always check with each other if your child has a complaint about the other parent. Children's perceptions are often skewed and stories tend to grow as they are repeated to other people. Sometimes this is intentional and other times it is not. Always consult the other parent if the child is complaining about something serious before flying off the handle.
- The parent with the child at the time is responsible for transporting him or her to scheduled activities, such as sports, classes, etc.
- Decide who will be responsible for your child's meal if transfer time is scheduled near a normal meal time.

Think about other ground rules you will need to have in place to make you comfortable in exercising your visitation and add those that are helpful to your specific situation. You probably know the other parent's hot spots. Try to avoid setting each other off and make some rules to help you do this.

Give and Take

Flexibility is a must in making the schedule work. Think of living with the schedule as a give-and-take situation and not as giving in, letting the other parent win, or being victorious. If you let the other parent change weekends with you this time, then when you ask for a change the next time, it shouldn't be a problem. This might mean you and the other parent will have to acknowledge and accept that you both have separate lives now, and that won't be easy!

This does not mean you should make changes on a regular basis. Your child needs stability. But some changes are okay. Do not feel that just because the judge told you to begin visitation at 5:30 p.m. on Wednesdays that it is written in stone. You and the other parent can make any adjustments to the schedule as long as you both agree to do so. If 6:00 p.m. works better for both of you, then make that your scheduled time. Be prepared to have to make adjustments as your life, the other parent's life, and your child's life change and grow. The schedule needs to develop as your lives do.

Create a Written Schedule

Even if you have a court-ordered schedule, you should still put it on a calendar so you both have a written schedule of where your child will be when. Make the schedule for the whole year, but do it in pencil. Then look at it and talk about what needs to be changed. If you have to go out of town during one of your scheduled weekends, or if the other parent wants a weekend alone to prepare for an exam, make adjustments. Look at how the holidays will be divided and talk about whether they will work the way they are currently scheduled, and make adjustments as needed. If you have the right to a week or so of vacation with your child, try to plan out when you are going to take it at this time.

Bite Your Tongue

The most important thing to remember when dealing with the other parent is to think before you speak. Try not to have knee-jerk responses to the things about him or her that irritate you. Try not to get angry or upset in front of the other parent. Go home and punch your pillow or scream in the shower afterwards, but do not get into confrontations. Your time with your child is very important to you. Think of the other parent as a hurdle you must get over to achieve it. You are going to have emotions, but you must do your best to not let them control you. Time with your child is your prize. This does not mean you have to be a victim or give in on every point. Choose your battles carefully and try to minimize them. Be polite and courteous to the other parent, even if you do not get the same treatment in return.

Never, ever argue in front of your child if you can help it. Your child is already struggling to believe that the divorce or breakup is not his or her fault. When parents argue about visitation, all the child thinks is that *they are arguing because of me.* Table all disagreements to be handled when your child is not around.

COMMUNICATION RULES

➤ *Do not yell.* The best way to communicate with the other parent is by using a neutral, calm voice. Raising your voice will lead to an argument.

➤ *Be clear about what you are talking about.* Try to address only one issue at a time. Do not confuse things by bringing up other topics or problems.

➤ *Let the past go.* Don't try to discuss what has happened in the past with your relationship. Focus on the present and the future with regard to your child.

➤ *Repeat yourself if necessary.* Sometimes you may try to discuss an issue relating to visitation and the other parent will try to bring up other things—child support, arguments over possessions, etc. If you respond, you will both

continued...

---

be diverted from the important issue at hand—time with your child. Repeat your question or comment calmly until he or she answers. You can also say that you are not willing to talk about the other issue now and want only to talk about the visitation issue.

➤ *Choose your times.* If you want to have a discussion with the other parent, do so at a time when you are both able to talk freely and are not rushed or tired.

➤ *Try to talk in "I" phrases instead of "you" phrases.* If you are having a problem with visitation, say things like, "I am having trouble picking Trevor up at 4 p.m. Could we change it to 5 p.m.?" Avoid saying things like, "You are going to have change the time we exchange Trevor." Try to focus the sentence on your needs, your problem, or your situation, and avoid sentences that sound like accusations, criticisms, or complaints.

➤ *Do not discuss things you don't need to.* This means letting some things go and focusing on the important issues. Do you really need to discuss whether or not your child watched tv after 9 p.m. at the other parent's house? Probably not, unless there is an ongoing problem. Choose your issues and let the smaller ones go.

➤ *Speak with respect.* Remember, he or she is your child's other parent and is extremely important to your child. This is the person you created life with. He or she deserves to be treated with respect, even if you believe that he or she is truly not worthy of it.

Having Meetings

Some parents find that they are best able to communicate with each other if they schedule a weekly or monthly meeting or phone call to discuss their child. Do so when you can talk without your child overhearing. Talk about problems that have come up, schedule changes that need to be made, reactions your child is having, and things coming up in the future. Speak calmly and rationally, pushing aside all of those emotions that will get in the way of your objective.

If child support needs to be discussed, do so either at the end of the meeting or at an entirely different time.

The need for such formal meetings will dissipate the longer you are divorced, and you will eventually learn to have quick unscheduled phone calls, emails, or chats. There may be times when large problems develop in the future, and you might find that resuming a regular meeting or schedule can help.

A Mediator Can Help

If you are having trouble communicating with each other (after all, old habits are hard to break), consider seeing a mediator who can help you work through the issues and develop a new way to talk to each other without arguments. It really is possible. Your local bar association or the *Association for Conflict Resolution* (202-464-9700, **www.acrnet.org**) can help you find a mediator. A mediator is a neutral third party who helps you and the other parent work through problems yourselves. If you and the other parent find you are completely unable to solve conflicts, a mediator can help solve the problems at hand and teach you how to resolve problems that may arise in the future.

Taking the Business Transaction Approach

If you have tried working together, if you have tried biting your tongue, and none of it has worked—if you and the other parent are at each other's throats and cannot agree on anything—think of your dealings with the other parent as a business transaction. Be polite, but do not argue or display emotion. Communicate by written notes or email if you cannot talk. You want to accomplish the task of arranging a schedule and exchanging your child.

You have to go through the checkout line at the grocery store before you can take the food home. Things go more quickly if you cooperate with the cashier. If you argue and bicker, you may never be handed that grocery bag. Think of the other parent like a cashier—a person you must deal with to arrange time with your child. He or she may not want you to have time with your child and may do everything possible to thwart you. Rise to the challenge. Refuse to be deterred. Time with your child is more rewarding and important than anything you have ever strived for. Your job is to make sure you get time with your child using every civil means at your disposal.

If you have to stand at the door and listen to the tirade when you pick up your son or daughter, do it! It may be a pain in the neck, but it is worth it to be able to spend time with your child. However, if the other parent is actively trying to prevent you from having time with your child (taking your son or daughter away over your weekend, not being home when you come for pick-up, etc.), you need to talk to your lawyer and consider seeking assistance from the court.

7

COPING
WITH VISITATION

You used to live in the same house with your child and your activities together developed naturally. Now when you see your child, everything feels artificial. Lots of nonresidential parents feel the same way—you're not alone. It can be hard to figure out how to have a normal life with your child when you see each other on a schedule that makes everything seem so artificial. The first thing to do is just relax! You and your child love each other. It really doesn't matter what you actually do, as long as you are spending time together. As you go along, it really will get easier. Remember, of course, that you may experience bumps in the road as your child ages and as situations change. Come back to this chapter for help at those times.

Changing How You Think

The idea of visitation with your own child is a ridiculous concept. Parents do not visit with their children. Parents live with their children. This is how you need to think about time with your child—a period of time when you and your child are living together, even if it is only for a few hours or for a weekend. Your child has two parents who no longer live in the same home, so you each must take turns living with the child. It doesn't matter how little time you have with your child, it is still a period of time when you are living together as a family unit.

You Are Not an Entertainer

Many nonresidential parents feel as if they must entertain their children when they are together (often called the *Disneyland Dad Syndrome*). When you lived in the same house with your child, were you responsible for his or her constant entertainment? Of course not. You were two people, living under the same roof, who shared some activities. This isn't going to be as easy now simply because your time together is scheduled, feels more formal, and is shorter. Some changes will be necessary, but overall it is important that you continue to have the attitude that you are living together, and that your time together is not some sacred institution that must be recognized with continual exciting events and fast food dinners. You need to get back to being comfortable with each other.

Staying Home

Just because it is your scheduled time with your child does not mean you need to have a list a mile long of places to go and things to do together. Many nonresidential parents over-schedule because they are afraid they will run out of things to do. This is your child. You'll never run out of things to do together! You can just *be* together sometimes. You don't need to be afraid of down time. It's okay to just hang around together sometimes.

You need to make time for you and your child to be at home—at your home—together. Your child needs to believe that he or she is still part of your life and that your home is his or her home. To do this, you need to learn to share the space together.

Continuing Daily Activities

It is important to make the time you spend together feel comfortable and natural. If your child spends the night at your home, you shouldn't jump out of bed early and cook a huge breakfast, unless this is something you would normally do. Don't rent 5 DVDs or make plans to have a heart-to-heart chat unless this is something you normally would have done. Get out of bed when you normally would, eat together, watch TV together, play some games, but also allow for some alone time. You can be in the same home without constantly interacting with each other. It's okay to answer the phone, take out the trash, read the paper, or do your hair, but make sure you don't ignore your child. The fact that you are able to act naturally will reassure your child and let him or her know that this is a real home and not a vacation spot.

Making Your Child Part of Your Home

Your child now has two homes. Make your child comfortable in your home by giving him or her a bedroom or at least some space to call his or her own. Encourage your child to arrange and decorate the room as it suits him or her. Do not splurge or overspend on the set up of this room. Buy or borrow what is needed to make it comfortable and livable within your budget. Purchasing one or two special things is fine, but your goal is not to make this your child's fantasy room to compensate for the divorce or separation, or to try to convince him or her it would be better to live with you.

Encourage your child to really live in your home—by using the TV, the stereo, the dishwasher, the shower, having friends over, and so forth. Expect your child to clean up his or her own messes and perform some household chores. This is an important part of really feeling ownership in the space.

Refer to the home as *our* home not as *my* home. Your home will always be your child's home, even if he or she isn't there all the time.

Sitters

There will come a time when you will need to go somewhere or do something without your child during your scheduled parenting time (such as a doctor's appointment, an important meeting, a funeral, etc). This is perfectly acceptable, as long it is not something that happens every time.

If your child is young enough to need a sitter, you will need to make arrangements for one. What did you and the other parent do when you were together and needed a sitter? Maybe there was a relative or friend who stayed with your child, or perhaps you hired a sitter. You will need to decide what will work best in your situation and what will help your child feel most comfortable. Consider asking the other parent to step in while you are away as another option. Some parents have a standing agreement that they will always ask the other parent to babysit before locating a sitter.

Finding New Things to Do

This is your big chance to expand your child's horizons. Have you always wanted to take your child to fly a kite? Do you think your child might be interested in starting a collection of some kind? Try new things a little at a time and see how you both like them. You can do things that you never would have been able to do with the other parent along. Don't be afraid to give new things a chance. If your child doesn't enjoy something, don't do it again—but you might find you have stumbled upon a great new activity for just the two of you to do together. Give both your child and yourself permission to experiment and try new things together.

Dealing with Belongings

When parents have disputes about parenting time, one of the biggest points of contention is about the child's other belongings. In the big scheme of things, clothes, toys, and belongings should not really be so important that they disrupt everyone's lives. You and the other parent should resolve not to let disagreements about stuff trip you up. As a practical matter, managing stuff can be quite time consuming and can cause a lot of disruption if it is not handled in an organized way.

Allow your child to bring some belongings from the other parent's home if the other parent agrees. Bringing a few things that mean home will go a long way toward helping your child adjust, and this is true for children of all ages. It is also a good idea for your child to leave some extra clothes at your home or to purchase some with you to leave there. You also need to make sure that there are toys, books, a toothbrush, hair spray, shampoo, videos, favorite foods, pencils, paper, bottles or sippy cups for toddlers or preschoolers, and other items for your child to use at your home. It is hard to cart these things back and forth all the time, so you need to have some items just for your home.

There are some items that will travel back and forth with the child—special toys, blankets, expensive items such as CD players and CDs, as well as school books, sports equipment, and musical instruments. Items such as outerwear and shoes also will travel with the child. Discuss what these items are with the child and the other parent. From the beginning, you and your child need to find a way to get organized about what needs to travel with the child. Keep a list on the refrigerator of these items or store the items in a particular place, such as next to the front door, so they will always be together and won't be forgotten. If something important is left behind, make arrangements for the child to get it. You may wish to use a marker chart so the list can remain permanent. You can mark items off in erasable marker each time.

SAMPLE LIST OF BELONGINGS THAT TRAVEL WITH YOUR CHILD

Infant or Toddler
- ❏ snowsuit/coat
- ❏ clothes
- ❏ blanket
- ❏ pacifier
- ❏ special toys
- ❏ medication
- ❏ any bottles, cups, or dishes that came with the child
- ❏ diaper bag

School-Age Child
- ❏ backpack
- ❏ homework
- ❏ books
- ❏ sneakers
- ❏ bag of clothes
- ❏ sports uniform/equipment
- ❏ computer disks (for homework)
- ❏ assignment notebook

continued...

❒ stuffed animals, action figures, or toys
❒ instrument
❒ hand-held video games
❒ favorite pillow
❒ lunchbox
❒ coat
❒ boots/shoes
❒ medication
❒ laminated card with both parents' information:
    ❒ phone numbers
    ❒ cell phone numbers
    ❒ pagers
    ❒ email addresses

Teen.

❒ cosmetics and other hygiene items that he or she is particular about
❒ hair brush
❒ personal CD player
❒ CDs
❒ computer disks and games
❒ homework and school books
❒ backpack
❒ coat
❒ uniform and equipment
❒ diary or journal
❒ boots/shoes
❒ bag of clothes and accessories
❒ cell phone
❒ medication
❒ personal organizer
❒ instrument
❒ laptop
❒ wallet or purse
❒ MP3 player

Laundry is a heated point of contention with some parents. The best policy is to return the clothes that belong at the other house laundered, if possible. Discuss this with the other parent. Older children can take on this responsibility themselves.

Going Out

Just as you did when you lived under the same roof, sometimes you will want to go out with your child. Plan things that you will both enjoy, but remember not to overplan. Get input from your child about where he or she would like to go. Be sure to include visits to your family. Children need to remain connected to their extended families. Choose age-appropriate activities and do not plan to do too much. If you have your child with you for a weekend, one event or big outing is plenty. Continue to do normal errands and outings as needed. Simply riding in the car together is a great opportunity to talk and be together.

Ideas for Activities

It can be hard to decide what you should be doing together during visitation. This section will offer suggestions to give you some ideas. Additionally, you should remember that your child may have activities, such as sports practice or a friend's birthday party, scheduled during your time. Make sure you plan around these.

You may also want to talk to the other parent about sharing responsibility for some appointments or regular events. For example, if you were the one who always took your child for haircuts, perhaps you would like to continue doing this. Talk to the other parent and decide who will be handling which appointments. Some parents decide that one parent will take the child shopping for new shoes while the other will take the child shopping for new coats. Doing these things will keep you involved in your child's life. Certainly, they are not the most exciting ways to spend time together, but they are normal and can help both of you feel normal too. If you don't feel comfortable doing these things or don't feel that you want to use up your time together in this way, that's okay too.

For more creative and fun ideas, get some books from the library with children's games or crafts that are appropriate for your child, if this is something you would enjoy doing together. Have some toys, books, and games on hand that your child will be interested in. Talk to other divorced or separated parents about things they do with their children. Search online for crafts, projects, quizzes, and other activities you can do together. Pick up a copy of your local parenting magazine. (Find yours online at **www.parentingpublications.org**.) These magazines list activities that are happening in your community or city that are appropriate for families. Your local newspaper will list movies, community events, and review restaurants that may be appropriate for children. Check out websites for your area for other happenings.

You will probably find that as you have more time alone with your child, you will find more and more things to do together and you will be willing to try things that you never would have when you lived together. Remember to be yourself, and if you are not comfortable with the thought of a certain activity or outing, then just don't plan it. If you are simply terrified of water, then it is silly to plan to take your child fishing. Your child loves you for who you are, not for the things you plan.

Try some of the following ideas for things to do together when you feel as if you are in a rut. Ideas are included for all age categories. Choose those that seem right for your child.

THINGS TO DO AT HOME WITH YOUR CHILD

- Play cards or a board game
- Do a word or jigsaw puzzle
- Build a model from a kit
- Paint or draw
- Take a walk
- Rent a movie
- Play a computer or video game
- Make a snowman
- Rearrange the furniture
- Make a scrapbook of your time together
- Cook something together
- Look at old photographs from your childhood
- Play charades
- Do a craft project together
- Toss a ball around outside
- Draw your dream houses
- Make up a story together
- Brush the dog
- Fold the laundry
- Do yoga, tae kwon do, or other exercises
- Wash the dishes or clean
- Dance
- Get a pet
- Read aloud to each other
- Invite family members over
- Invite one of your child's friends over to play or visit
- Plan a party or vacation
- Plant a garden
- Listen to music and sing off-key
- Go for a bike ride
- Draw with chalk
- Do car repairs together
- Build something with wood
- Make milk carton villages
- Go through boxes of your old school memories
- Watch birds
- Play with toys
- Design a family crest
- Build a robot
- Paint the child's room
- Use a telescope
- Tell knock-knock jokes
- Tell your child stories about him- or herself
- Play hide-and-go-seek
- Talk about what's happening at school or in the news
- Start a journal that you take turns writing in
- Surf the Internet
- Do homework (You do some of your work while your child does school work, or assist your child when needed.)
- Plan a vacation together
- Watch TV and talk about what you are watching
- Play house
- Make a tent with blankets
- Design a calendar together
- Start a stamp collection
- Research bugs
- Take photographs of each other
- Paint a room
- Research the meanings of your names
- Research your family history or genealogy

IDEAS FOR OUTINGS WITH YOUR CHILD

- Go to the park
- Take a spur-of-the-moment overnight trip somewhere
- Go to the library
- Go to a make-your-own-pottery shop
- Go to a movie
- Eat out—try new places and different foods
- Go to a tennis court
- Join a parent/child book club
- Go to a basketball court
- Do volunteer work together
- Watch a sporting event
- Pick your own fruit
- Get a makeover
- Go to the beach
- Get your hair cut together
- Go to an amusement park
- Visit friends
- Go to a carnival
- Take a tour of your own city
- Go shopping
- Drive by all the places you used to live
- Go to a museum
- Fly a kite
- Walk around city hall
- Ride a bus or the subway
- Visit the newborn nursery at the hospital where your child was born
- Go to a video arcade
- Go camping, even if for an afternoon
- Pick flowers or collect rocks
- Visit a nearby town or city
- Visit an animal shelter
- Go to the zoo
- Take a nature walk
- Go sledding
- Take a class together (such as art, karate, dance, horseback riding, etc.)
- Go hiking
- Go skiing
- Go bike riding
- Go roller blading
- Attend local puppet shows and children's performances
- Go canoeing
- Attend story time at a library or bookstore
- Browse around a book or music store
- Go ice skating
- Bring your child to your office
- Join the Y and work out or swim there
- Play laser tag
- Visit relatives
- Hang out with friends who have kids the same age
- Go on a picnic
- Go grocery shopping for a meal you plan to make together
- Go to the mall
- Go roller blading
- Go fishing
- Attend a concert

Vacations

Your parenting plan may include a long period of time each year for you and your child to vacation together. Remember that you do not have to actually go anywhere during this time. Staying at home is absolutely fine. You should try, however, to arrange your schedule so you can spend a large portion of this time with your child.

If you do decide to travel or go somewhere, give the other parent a phone number where you can be reached, as well as the dates you will be gone. Try to involve your child in planning the trip. Give your child the opportunity to call the other parent while you are away. If this is the first time your young child has been away from the other parent for an extended period of time, expect there to be some separation anxiety. Deal with it by being loving and tolerant, allowing contact with the other parent by phone or Internet, and by simply using distraction.

You may feel nervous or apprehensive about spending a long period of time alone with your child. It may take some adjustment, but you and your child really will be fine together. Try not to have high expectations and be patient.

Getting Help

If you've read this chapter and you still feel overwhelmed or scared about actually parenting alone, don't worry. First of all, almost all nonresidential parents have these feelings and almost all of them manage to do just fine. If you still really feel like you just cannot do this, there is help. Look first to your own family. Spend some time with your child visiting your own parents. Grandparents love to see their grandchildren and feel quite comfortable helping out. Having your own parents there might help you relax a bit as well. If your parents aren't available, try other close relatives. Remember that this is okay to do once in a while, but you need to work up to the point where you do spend time with your child alone.

If you have friends with children close in age to your child, get together with them. The kids can play together and you can get some support from your friends. Find out if there are any single parent clubs or Mommy and me/Daddy and me get-togethers in your area. Being with other parents of the same sex who are spending time with their children can help you cope. Often, these kinds of support groups can be wonderful for you and your child and help give you a sense of community.

Look in your local newspaper, magazines, on websites about your area, and on bulletin boards at churches, synagogues, community centers, and fitness clubs to find these kinds of groups. Also, do not be afraid to join a group of parents of the opposite sex. Always ask if you are welcome first, but you will probably find that single parents are very supportive of each other, no matter what the sex. There are also many online support groups. (See Appendices B and C for information about these.)

When You *Don't* Need Help

There may come a time where you feel as if the other parent is being a little too overbearing and a little too helpful. If he or she is sending the child with detailed schedules and notes on a regular basis, is calling to check in too often, and is really giving you the impression that he or she does not think you can handle things, it might make you feel angry, insulted, frustrated, and offended.

The best way to handle this kind of problem is to find a good time to talk to the other parent (when your child is not around). Explain that you appreciate the help he or she is trying to give, but it is making you feel as if he or she does not trust you with the child. Say that you always want to know what is going with your child and you always want there to be an open line of communication, but you don't need detailed instructions and tips. Explain that you and your child are doing really well together, and if there is ever a problem, question, or concern, you will be sure to call—but until then, you really need some space. If he or she persists in sending you these instructions, stop reading them if it really makes you upset (but realize that you do run the risk of not reading something that could be important).

You probably have a lot more that you want to say to the other parent about this, but if you look at it rationally, shouting, getting angry, or starting an argument is not going to help anything. You want to reassure the other parent that you are capable of parenting without constant instructions and input, and you aren't going to effectively do so if you lose your temper.

If the other parent calls too frequently to check on the child at your house, you need to have a discussion about limiting the calls. Set a limit of one call every four hours (or use any time frame that you think is reasonable). You don't want to get to the point where he or she calls and you simply stop answering. This will cause the other parent to panic. If you have an answering machine picking up the calls, it will make your child wonder why you aren't letting him or her talk to Mommy or Daddy. Remember that the other parent may act over-protectively as a reaction to visitation, but that this normally will decrease as everyone adjusts.

Easing Transitions

For most children, the transition from one parent to another is the most difficult part of visitation. When you pick up your child or drop him or her off, expect there to be some difficulties. To make transitions easier when you pick up your child, you should talk about what you have planned and what you will be doing that day. When you are dropping off your child, talk about what he or she will be doing with the other parent and when he or she will see you next. Transitions are hard with older kids and teens as well; they may close up or become shy.

Many parents find that the most difficult part of their time with their children is the time at the beginning and end of their scheduled time. It is hard for children to leave one parent and instantly get into the groove with the other. When your time begins, give each other a little space to adjust without immediately jumping into an intense activity together. Allow your child time to unpack or get a snack if you are at home, or time to adjust to the surroundings if you are in public.

To ease the transition at the end of your time together, tell the child in advance when the time will be up and give some additional reminders, such as two hours before, one hour before, and half an hour before. Make sure that when you part, you are able to point to the next time you will be together and make some reference to what you will be doing together then. Also point out if you will have phone or email contact before then. This emphasizes the ongoing nature of your relationship and provides a viable link to your next time together.

Some parents find that transitions can be eased if the parent the child is currently with transports him or her to the other parent. So, the other parent would bring the child to you and you would return him or her. Transitioning in a public place such as a park, a mall, or a restaurant, can also make things easier. It may also be easier if you do not transition directly with the other parent. Try picking your child up at school and returning him or her there the next school morning.

If transitioning is still difficult, you could try using a relative or friend as a transition person. The other parent could drop your child off at Grandma's house and you could pick him or her up there. This can be especially effective if you and the other parent can't seem to exchange your child without an argument.

TRANSITIONING TIPS

➤ Transition in a public place or at a relative's home.

➤ Use the beginning or ending of school as a transition time so the child does not go directly from one parent to the other.

➤ Don't shoehorn your child from one parent's car to the other's. Spend a few minutes somewhere before popping him or her back in a car.

➤ Tell your child a joke or a funny story.

➤ Remind him or her when you will be together again, or if it is the beginning of your time, remind him or her when he or she will be with the other parent next.

➤ Give him or her some space to adjust. Allow some quiet, individual time before getting into an activity together.

continued...

> Keep your thoughts or complaints about the other parent under wraps. Don't use transition time to have a discussion or argument with the other parent.
> Be polite and friendly to the other parent. Smile!
> Try not to rush. Being frantic just makes things worse.
> If hugging and kissing is natural for you, do it!
> Make it clear you are happy to see your child when your time together begins.
> Do not be disappointed if your child does not act happy to see you.

Dealing with Medication

If your child needs to be given any medication while at your house, it is a good idea to keep track of when you have given it and how much. This helps you keep track and also lets the other parent know what was given when, which is important if further doses are going to be given on a proper schedule. Do this for nonprescription and prescription medications. Use a dosage chart to record the medications given. When your child comes to stay with you, make sure you find out when the last dose was given so you can give the next dose at the appropriate time.

SAMPLE DOSAGE CHART

Date	Time	Name of Medication	Amount Given
————	————	————————————	————————
————	————	————————————	————————
————	————	————————————	————————
————	————	————————————	————————

Keeping Track of Feeding and Sleeping

If your child is a baby or toddler, it is a good idea if you and the other parent can share information about when he or she ate or slept last, so that the other parent has an idea of what to expect. Use this chart to help track this.

SLEEP SCHEDULE

Date	Time	Woke Up At	Notes

FEEDING SCHEDULE

Date	Time	Amount	Notes

Interference With Your Scheduled Time

Unfortunately, there are some residential parents who try to sabotage or interfere with the nonresidential parent's time. If you suspect this is your situation, first try to take a hard look at what is happening. Are you misinterpreting things? Are you being overly sensitive? If not, and the other parent is truly doing things that interfere with your visitation, try to talk to him or her calmly. Explain how important visitation is to your child and how all children need two parents. Explain that you are not trying to interfere in the other parent's life, make things difficult for him or her, or hurt anyone's feelings by spending time with your child. You just love your child and want to spend time with him or her. It has nothing to do with your relationship with the other parent. Talk about ways to solve the problems you are experiencing. Maybe a schedule change would help things, or perhaps the other parent is upset about things you are unaware of, or he or she is misinterpreting things. The only way to get to the bottom of this is to communicate with each other.

If none of this helps and the other parent continues to deny you time with your child at your scheduled times or is consistently late getting the child to you, you need to speak to your attorney. A residential parent must not interfere with visitation, and in some instances, doing so can be grounds for a change in custody.

8

SCHEDULING

One of the hardest things to deal with once you are divorced or separated is learning to live with seeing your child on a schedule. Most parents are used to just seeing their child whenever they are home. Parenting on a schedule is a learned skill. It takes time to get used to living by the schedule and to learn how to manage a schedule. Once you become accustomed to it, things will go much more smoothly.

Dealing with the Schedule

Most parents have a schedule that is set by the court or agreed to by both parents. This schedule can be adjusted if both you and the other parent agree to alter it. See Chapter 6 for more information about creating and modifying the schedule with the other parent. Once the schedule is set, it is important that both you, the other parent, and your child have it on a calendar. There is nothing worse than forgetting to pick up your child because you got your days mixed up.

When you create a schedule, it is a good idea to have some basic rules to prevent confusion. You can set up a rule that the other parent will always bring the child to you and you will return him or her. You can agree that whomever has the child at 6:00 p.m. will provide dinner, and so on. These basic rules allow you to avoid constant negotiations about routine daily events.

SAMPLE SCHEDULING RULES

➤ Changes to the schedule require 24 hours notice, except in emergencies.

➤ The parents will try to accommodate reasonable schedule change requests made by each other.

➤ If the parent providing transportation will be late, he or she will call as soon as possible to let the other parent and child know.

➤ Each parent will be assigned pick-up and drop-off duties that will remain the same. Pick-ups and drop-offs will be at a set time. For example, Parent A will always drop off the child at 7 p.m. every other Friday, and Parent B will always drop off the child at 2 p.m. every other Sunday. These times will not change unless the parents agree.

➤ The parents will meet or talk once a month to exchange scheduling information.

➤ The nonresidential parent will contact the school and extracurricular activities leaders for copies of calendars and schedules. If a calendar change notice is sent home with the child, it will be shared with the nonresidential parent.

➤ Schedule change requests will be made directly by one parent to the other and messages will not be carried by the child.

➤ If the child has a scheduled activity planned during visitation, the nonresidential parent will transport the child (if needed) to and from the activity.

➤ The nonresidential parent shall have the right to have the child skip a normally planned activity scheduled during his or her visitation time if he or she has a more important, one-time event planned.

➤ Each parent will maintain a calendar and keep track of visitation times and the child's activities.

➤ An age appropriate calendar will be maintained for the child's use.

You also need to help your child learn to live by the schedule. Create a calendar for the child with the schedule clearly marked. For young children, a color-coded calendar is very helpful. Color Mom's days blue and Dad's days red (or any colors you choose) and on the transition days, split the day in half with a color on each side. Older children can use a calendar that has pick-up and drop-off times written on it. Teens may wish to incorporate the schedule into their school calendar, or on their computers or organizers.

Incorporating Your Child's Events

It is important for you to remember that your child has a schedule of his or her own. Many children participate in after school-activities and have various lessons and classes to attend. You need to obtain copies of all correspondence that deals with your child's schedule. Request that coaches, teachers, group leaders, etc., send you a copy of all calendars or scheduling items. Most are willing to make sure you get a second copy. Sometimes this information is just sent home with the child. You and the other parent need to agree that whomever receives this information should share it with the other parent. Make sure you obtain a copy of the school calendar from the main office, as well as notification about field trips and other special events. Mark all of these on your calendar, even if they are happening on a day when you won't be with your child. (Your parenting schedule could change and you might need this information.) Talk to the other parent and make sure you are told about medical or dental appointments, special occasions, and so on, that are scheduled for your child, particularly if they fall during your regular visitation.

Time for Friends

When kids reach elementary school, friends become more important. Encourage your child to invite friends to your home on occasion. You should also let your child know that you don't object to him or her visiting friends occasionally during your parenting time, as long as it doesn't use up the entire time. Getting to know your child's friends and encouraging your child to spend time with them will bring you closer together. Teens are another story entirely. (See Chapter 13 for more information about dealing with teens and their friends.)

Working Out Problems

Many parents feel torn when faced with a conflict between parenting time and a scheduled activity of the child's. When you lived under the same roof, did you tell your son he could not go to little league practice because it was your night with him? Did you suggest your daughter skip the prom because it was your weekend? You need to continue to allow your child to participate in activities that are important to him or her. If you require a child to skip an activity, all you will get out of it is resentment.

Remember that when you are with your child, your goal is to live with him or her. So if your child has an activity on your night, drive him or her there, pick him or her up afterwards, or be at home with him or her before and after the event or activity. Have some dinner before or afterwards and fit in whatever else you can. Not only will your child be able to have the continuity and support these activities provide, but you will get to be involved with them.

If you find that there are too many conflicts with your parenting time, then you and the other parent need to rearrange the schedule while taking into consideration the child's schedule. Try to balance things out so that scheduled activities do not take huge chunks of time away from either of you.

Saying No

Although it is important for your child to continue sports and activities that are fun and enriching, there does come a time when you should say no. If your child is scheduled for something every single day, it might be time to talk to the other parent and the child about cutting back. If you and your child have something important planned (such as a camping trip together or your grandmother's 90th birthday party) that conflicts with your child's planned activity, you are using your authority as a parent when you decide the child will have to miss the activity just once. Be sure to explain this calmly to your child and inform the other parent.

Making Changes to Your Life

You may find that it is unrealistic for you to see your child every Wednesday evening as your parenting plan calls for. Maybe you are finding that you just can't pick him or her up for weekends at 5:30 on Friday as scheduled.

If this is the case, can the parenting schedule be changed so that you can get as much time, just on different days? That is the ideal situation. If this won't work, then you need to make some life choices. If time with your child is more important to you than your job or time with your friends, perhaps you can make some changes in those areas of your life. It might be possible, for instance, to work more hours on Tuesday so you can leave work earlier on Wednesday. You could make arrangements to date only on alternate weekends if you are having conflicts with your social life.

Remember that you are permitted to make changes to the parenting schedule only if both you and the other parent agree. This is not something you can do on your own. Realize that you may have to make some sacrifices from time to time in order to make parenting a priority.

Maximizing Visitation Time

You have a set schedule you are supposed to follow. Look at your schedule and figure out approximately how many days or hours the schedule gives you with your child in a week or in a month. If changes are made to the schedule, you should still end up with roughly the same amount of time. If you are normally scheduled alternate weekends from 7 p.m. on Friday to 2 p.m. on Sunday, and an alteration is made so you can't pick up your child until 9 p.m. on Friday, then technically, you should change the Sunday time to 4 p.m., or add two hours somewhere else.

This can get very nit-picky if you try to be militant about it. Look to see that you are getting roughly the same amount of time each month. A few hours here or there aren't going to make a huge difference, but if you are losing a lot of time on a consistent basis, you need to speak up to the other parent and ask that the time be made up somehow.

Understanding Some Schedule Basics

Sometimes talking about schedules can get confusing. If you are supposed to have your child every other weekend, for example, this means that you have the child weekend A, the other parent has the child weekend B, then it is your turn again weekend C, and so on. If you and the other parent agree to swap weekends, things can get confusing. If the normal schedule of weekends is:

>Weekend A: you
>Weekend B: the other parent
>Weekend C: you
>Weekend D: the other parent

and you and the other parent agree that you are going to swap weekends A and B, then the new schedule would be:

>Weekend A: the other parent
>Weekend B: you
>Weekend C: you
>Weekend D: the other parent

Don't get confused and think that weekend C should be the other parent's since you are on an alternating schedule. You substituted weekend B for weekend A, which was your regularly scheduled weekend. Weekend C is your next regularly scheduled weekend. The same applies if the other parent ends up with two weekends in row because of a change.

Another point of confusion is holidays. If your holiday falls on a weekend or a day that is your regularly scheduled time, you will get your holiday and regularly scheduled time simultaneously. You don't get extra time. If it is your holiday and it falls during the other parent's time, you get the time and the other parent does not. If it is the other parent's holiday and it falls during your regular visitation time, the other parent gets the child for the holiday. Holidays trump regularly scheduled time.

If your holiday falls on a weekend or time the child is normally scheduled to be with the other parent, you will get that holiday and you will then see the child on your next regularly scheduled time—even if this means you get two weekends in a row. For example:

> Weekend A: your regular time
> Weekend B: the other parent's regular time, but it is Christmas and it is your turn to have it, so the child will be with you
> Weekend C: your regular time
> Weekend D: the other parent's regular time

Keep in mind that this can work the other way too—the other parent may end up having the child for two or three weekends some years because a holiday he or she is scheduled to have falls during your regular visitation time.

There can be confusion if your court-ordered schedule just says alternating holidays. You and the other parent need to sit down and work out what these holidays will be. You also want to be sure that you understand if you are alternating the holidays by year, for example:

> Last Year: your turn
> This Year: the other parent's turn
> Next Year: your turn

Or, if you are actually taking an every other holiday approach to things, for example:

> **This Year's Holiday Schedule**
> New Year's Day: your turn
> Easter: the other parent's turn
> Memorial Day: your turn
> Fourth of July: the other parent's turn
> Labor Day: your turn

This continues throughout the year, so that you have one holiday and the other parent gets the next one. This kind of schedule is hard to follow, especially if your family always celebrates on Christmas Eve and the other parent's family always celebrates on

Christmas Day, this kind of schedule could have your child missing both family celebrations.

Try to avoid these kinds of scheduling confusions by always writing schedules out on a calendar and being clear with the other parent about schedule changes.

Schedules Do Not Impact Child Support

Some parents mistakenly think that the amount of child support they pay is somehow related to the time their child is in the care of the other parent. For example, thinking that because you have your child for a week that you should not have to pay child support, since you are the one taking care of the child's needs for that week. Child support is an amount set by the court that must be paid regardless of how much time the child is with you. Child support is not related to your parenting schedule. Think of it separately.

If you and the other parent agree that the child should live primarily with you, then you need to speak to your attorney about having your child support payments eliminated and about getting child support from the other parent.

Schedule Violations

There will be times when both you and the other parent will make mistakes with regard to the schedule. Try to give each other some slack. No one is perfect and mistakes are going to happen. If you find that the other parent consistently makes mistakes about the schedule, first think about what kind of mistakes they are. Do these mistakes actually benefit you? For example, if the parent regularly picks your child up from visitation late, this actually gives you more time. You might not want to complain. However, this can be inconvenient if you have other things planned or other commitments to meet. If this is the case, or if the mistakes end up regularly cutting into your time, then you need to talk to the other parent. Explain that many mistakes are happening and you'd like to make sure that you both have the same dates or times written down. Suggest to the other parent that these mix-ups are confusing, frustrating, or upsetting for your child. Nicely ask if you can all try to stick to the schedule.

If this doesn't work, maybe you could make some permanent changes to the schedule. Perhaps the other parent is consistently late because he or she is getting caught in traffic or is getting out of work late. Changing the time should help eliminate the problem.

If none of this works, then you are going to have to tell the other parent that the schedule has to be followed, and if he or she refuses to, then you will have to call your attorney. Your attorney may be able to talk to the other parent's attorney and convince him or her to follow it, or you may have to go to mediation or to court as a last resort.

When Your Child Doesn't Want to Go

When the day comes when your child refuses to go with you during your scheduled time (and it happens in almost every family), you should not give in. No one wants to drag a child kicking and screaming with them, but the fact of the matter is you have a schedule, and everyone needs to follow it. Try to talk to the other parent if this kind of refusal is happening often. Ask for his or her help and support in getting your child to go. It's really important to present a united front when it comes to this. If the other parent does not insist your child go, then you look like the bad guy. It's also important to remember there may be a time when the situation is reversed and your child wants to stay with you and not return to the other home as scheduled. It is important that both you and the other parent stick to the schedule without giving in to these demands by your child.

Some parents feel that if a child doesn't want to go, he or she should not be forced to. There are certainly times when you should make changes in the schedule—when your child has an important activity, is too sick, or you have something important you need to do. But if you start letting your child decide at the last minute if he or she wants to go, you are giving him or her too much power and too much responsibility. It can become a game to see just how far he or she can push it. You and the other parent really need to be united about dealing with these refusals.

If the other parent is not helping the situation, stand your ground. This is your child's time with you. Part of being a parent is dealing with difficult times and stubborn kids. When you all lived together, if your child had refused to come out of his or her room and go to school, you would not have allowed it. This is the same kind of situation. To be a parent, you must have regular time with your child. Some of it might not be pleasant, but it's important for it to be regular.

If you can't get your child to go with you and the other parent won't help, let it go and try again next time. If you still get nowhere, it is time to talk to your attorney.

9

DEALING
WITH HOLIDAYS
AND CELEBRATIONS

Holidays are a very emotional time for divorced or separated people. They are even more difficult when children are in the equation. Your heart may ache at the thought of not being there when your child gets up on Christmas morning or at the thought of having no one to light the candles with on the menorah. Holidays are also difficult for the children of divorce. Children are sad and angry that both parents are not there. They are also sure they are hurting the parent they are not with. Try to remember how difficult the situation is for your child and for the other parent. Problems with holidays may pop up every year, so return to this chapter if you have problems in the future.

You shouldn't think of holidays as a time when you have to somehow compensate for the fact that you don't live with your child fulltime. Buying more gifts isn't going to make you a better parent or make your child love you more. Holidays can be a time for connecting with your child and finding meaningful activities, building memories, and creating new traditions together.

Dealing with Expectations
Whatever great or awful things you expect a holiday to bring, you are probably wrong! Expect it to be good and bad, but not the picture perfect festival or the absolute lonely disaster you are envi-

sioning. Be realistic about your expectations of yourself and of your child. View the holiday as another day that may have some nice components or some sad components to it.

Before a holiday comes around, take some time to talk about it with your child. Discuss whose house he or she will be at and talk about how you both feel about the plans. Let your child tell you what he or she likes or dislikes about the plan. Think of what you, your child, and the other parent can do to make the holiday go well.

The best way to ensure the holiday will go well is to think about giving your child the gift of happiness and love. You can give these things to your child no matter where he or she is. Focus on the joy a child deserves to experience, not on the loss or anger you feel. Let your child know that you love him or her and want him or her to have a good holiday, no matter where he or she is each year. Try to keep your perspective and don't get caught up in the craziness that holidays can bring.

Holidays when You are Together

When it is your turn to have your child for an important holiday, do not expect it to be of storybook quality. Your child may still feel strange in your home (if it is not the home you shared with the other parent) and may still be adjusting to the situation. Before the holiday, discuss your plans and let your child have some age-appropriate input. Make your child feel that he or she is an important part of the holiday by giving him or her some control over it. A 6-year-old could help decide where the Christmas tree should go, a 3-year-old could help decide what colors to use to decorate Easter eggs, and a teen could help prepare Thanksgiving dinner. Discuss what you and your child will be doing and make sure there is some time built into the schedule for a phone call between your child and the other parent, and possibly the other grandparents. It will be natural for your child to miss them and a phone call will help make contact again.

Your parenting plan probably has your child with the appropriate parent on Mother's Day or Father's Day. Enjoy your day and focus on your relationship with your son or daughter. That's what the day is all about, after all. Try to find happiness in your time together, no matter how short. Think of this as a day for celebrating motherhood or fatherhood and all the joys it has brought you.

One common problem on holidays together is when your child misses the other parent. This is no reflection on you or your relationship with your child. In fact, you can bet on the fact that when your child is with the other parent, he or she misses you. Let your child have phone contact with the other parent on the holiday. Don't be angry or hurt if you find out your child misses the other parent. Instead, accept it, tell your child you understand and you're sorry, and do what you can to make the day a good one.

HOLIDAY TRAPS TO AVOID

- *Making plans for every second.* Leave some down time for you and your child to spend together, or for your child to decompress alone.
- *Being overly festive.* Of course, you want to make the day special and you want your child to have fun, but too much gaiety can seem false. You also run the risk of making your child feel bad for not being equally thrilled.
- *Trying to follow the exact same traditions you used to follow as a family.* Nothing can ever truly be as it was and you only bring up bittersweet memories for both of you by trying to exactly recreate the past.
- *Completely reinventing the holiday.* Your child will want some things to be familiar and traditional. Pick some of the things you used to do as a family and incorporate them with some of your own new traditions to make it a special day.
- *Surrounding yourself with too many people.* You don't want your child to get lost in a crowd. Schedule some alone time.
- *Isolating yourselves.* If part of your holiday tradition involves visiting other family members, continue to do so. Focusing all of your time and attention on your child is too much pressure.

continued...

> ➤ *Doing the **remember when** routine.* A big part of holidays has to do with memories. It is okay to talk about a few things from the past, but in general, try to look forward. Looking back could easily make you both sad or angry if you dwell on it.
>
> ➤ *Becoming depressed.* It is natural for both you and your child to feel sad or angry because divorce or separation has changed your family. It is okay to be honest with your child ("It feels strange to me too not to have Daddy here"), but you should not unload your emotions ("I feel so alone because Mommy doesn't love me anymore"). Acknowledging the changed situation is okay, but dwelling on it is not.

Holidays Alone

Because you probably rotate or alternate holidays with the other parent, you will have to deal with spending a major holiday without your child at some point. It is easy to get wrapped up in the pain of spending a holiday alone. It is normal to feel abandoned, left out, and angry when you are unable to spend a holiday with your child. First, you need to find some way to get yourself through the day.

Tips for Handling Holidays Alone

➤ Spend time with friends or family.

➤ Attend a religious service if it is part of how you celebrate.

➤ Invite some people to a gathering at your home.

➤ Donate your time that day to a charity.

➤ Go to a movie and splurge on popcorn and candy.

➤ Rent a video.

➤ Curl up with a good book.

➤ Work on a home improvement project.

➤ Organize your photographs.

➤ Take a walk.

➤ Buy yourself a gift.

➤ Go to a parade, fireworks, or other community event.

➤ Cook yourself a special holiday meal.

➤ Clean your closets.

➤ Build a dollhouse or racetrack for your child.

➤ Rearrange the furniture.

➤ Visit an Internet chat room and talk to other parents in the same situation.

➤ Sleep in and eat breakfast in bed.

➤ Go away on a trip by yourself.

➤ Get that project done for work that you've been putting off.

➤ Go to a museum.

➤ Plant a garden.

➤ Take the time to start a hobby you've never tried.

➤ Perform a random act of kindness for a stranger.

➤ Go to the gym.

➤ Eat junk food.

➤ Go to bed early.

Find some way to be good to yourself that day. Feel free to acknowledge your feelings of sadness, anger, loss, and grief. Go ahead and wallow, cry, or yell. Your feelings are real and cannot be pushed aside.

Next, think about your child. Try to arrange for some telephone contact on the holiday. Touching base will make you both feel better. It is okay to tell your child how much you miss him or her, but do not make him or her feel sorry for you or guilty. Give your child permission to enjoy the day without you ("Have a good time at Grandma's house!" or "Have a great time opening those presents!").

If you haven't already done so, schedule an alternate time for you to celebrate the holiday with your child, such as the next day or on your next scheduled visitation. Remind your child of this during your phone call. Celebrate when you are next together. Even if it is not technically the holiday, it is *your* holiday. If you and the other parent are alternating holidays, remind yourself and your child that next year you will be together for this holiday.

When you talk to your child or see him or her, let him or her tell you about how he or she spent the holiday. Try to just listen without criticizing or making judgments. Comments like, "Your grandfather always lets you eat too much candy," will ruin your child's joy in the event. Be positive and let your child know you are happy he or she had a good day ("I'm glad you got that bicycle you've been wishing for!").

Holidays with the Other Parent

Many families find that in the first few years after a divorce or separation, the children are happiest if they can spend some time with their parents together on holidays. Some families spend part of Christmas morning together or share Thanksgiving dinner. If this is something you would like to do, discuss it with the other parent. You must both be comfortable and willing to make an arrangement like this work. If you do decide to try it, remember to keep things light. An argument will ruin the day.

Celebrating Birthdays

You may not see your child on his or her birthday because you and the other parent have agreed to alternate the day or because it falls on a day when you do not have visitation. Make contact with your child on the birthday—a phone call or a quick stop at the front door for a hug. Celebrate at the next opportunity. This is your child's special day. Do not let your problems with the other parent affect it.

Some families make a policy of having both parents present at birthday parties. If you and the other parent are both comfortable with this, give it a try. If not, you will need to discuss which parent will host a party for the child's friends. You can each have separate parties for your side of the family to celebrate.

Presents

Gift-giving can easily turn into a competition between parents. Each tries to give better, more expensive presents to prove he or she is the better parent. The best way to avoid this is to discuss it with the other parent. Some parents agree to discuss any purchases over a certain dollar amount with each other. Other parents give each other ideas about what each is buying so that there is little duplication. Others agree on a total amount each will not exceed. Like everything else involved with parenting together, things always work best when there is communication between the parents. Some parents even give some big, important gifts together. Do whatever works in your situation.

Avoid showering your child with gifts to make up for the time you spend apart. This strategy really does not work. Think about the amount and type of gifts your child received before the divorce or separation. Try to stick to the same plan. If you are purchasing a gift that will be primarily kept or used at your home, it is really your business and not the other parent's. However, think about how you would feel if you got your child a few small gifts, and then he or she went to the other parent's house and got a pony. If you're going to be buying an extravagant gift, it might be a good idea to let the other parent know. This might be something you could chip in for together. Even if you buy the gift alone, at least the other parent won't be shocked when he or she learns about it from your child.

All of this does not mean that you cannot buy your child that computer, video game system, or puppy he or she has been begging for. Try to discuss your plans with the other parent. If it is something your child really wants, it is unlikely the other parent will object, as long as he or she is not blindsided with it when the gift is given.

Where will your child keep the gifts you give him or her? You should decide ahead of time if you want the item to stay at your home or if your child can decide where to keep it.

Although it is unlikely you and the other parent will exchange holiday gifts, your child will certainly want to give the other parent a gift. You could take him or her shopping and let him or her buy a gift for the other parent or encourage a teen to do so. While you may have bad feelings toward the other parent, remember that your child loves him or her and sharing in the gift-giving will make your child feel happy. If you absolutely are not comfortable helping your child do this, try to see if some other family member can make sure your child has the opportunity to shop for both parents.

Staying on Track

There is generally an increase in parenting plan disputes at holiday times. Attorneys find themselves flooded with calls on the day before Thanksgiving, Christmas Eve, etc. Don't be one of the phone calls if you can help it. Try to work out disagreements calmly. However, if you are being denied your court assigned holiday time, definitely make a call to your attorney!

Don't let the holidays derail you. Constant court battles are usually not the answer. Find a way to work things out with the other parent. If you need help dealing with your emotions, see a counselor or therapist. Clergy are also experienced in dealing with holiday emotions and disputes. Do whatever you have to do to get through holidays. Remember that they come every year, so it is not the end of the world if you have a disappointing experience this year.

10

LONG-DISTANCE PARENTING

Some parents and children live in different cities, different states, or even different countries. Living far away from your child can be difficult for both of you, but it doesn't have to mean you can't have a close relationship.

Adjusting to a Long-Distance Relationship

If you or your child have recently moved away from each other, adjusting to this new kind of relationship is difficult. You may fear you will lose all closeness with your child, drift apart, or that your child will forget you. You may feel sadness and loss. Your child is having the same kinds of feelings. If he or she is the one moving, there may be resentment towards the other parent, who caused this move to happen. If you are the one moving, the resentment may be towards you.

It is important to remember that physical distance does not have to mean emotional distance. You must also keep in mind that whoever is moving away (whether it is your child or yourself) will be adjusting to a new home and new surroundings, as well as to this new long-distance relationship. There is a lot to adjust to when a move like this happens.

Many parents and children are able to maintain close relationships while living far apart. Take it one day at a time and try not to get overwhelmed. You are still an important part of your child's life, whether you live next door, in the next town, in the next state, or on the other coast.

Far, but not *that* Far

Some parents and children live several hours apart—just far enough to make frequent visits difficult, but close enough so that it is still possible to visit at least once a month. The best way to handle these kinds of visits is to arrange for larger blocks of time whenever possible. It is too much to ask of you and your child to commute this distance twice in one day. If you are limited to a visit that is relatively short, consider driving to the child's location and doing something there in your allotted time. Arrange for longer, overnight visits when possible.

Coping with Distance

Whether you or your child has recently moved away, or if you have lived apart for a while, distance is an obstacle in your relationship. The best way to cope with physical distance is to maintain an emotional closeness. This is very difficult to do with children who are under age 5 because they may not have the language or writing skills to communicate with you from far away. With young children, you need to send photographs and videos and talk to them on the phone, even if they do not respond. Ask the other parent to send you photos, videos, and drawings made by the child.

Older children can cope with distance a bit better by using technology to stay in touch. When you are geographically far apart, it is important to make an effort to have contact with your child on a frequent (at least twice a week) basis.

In-Person Visits

Your parenting plan probably allows for your child to have a long visit with you at least once a year. When planning a long visit, consider first the travel arrangements. Will the child be traveling alone or will you or someone else be with him or her? Airlines and trains will make arrangements for children who are traveling alone and provide personnel to escort them. Request assistance when the reservations are made. You could also travel one way with the child and let the other parent travel in the other direction. It may be most cost effective for the child to travel by car. If this is the case, each parent can drive the child in one direction. You may be in a situation where it is your responsibility to provide all of the transportation. Plan in advance and save money to cover airfare, or bring along a relative or friend to take turns driving. The cost of your child's transportation should be included in your parenting plan, so check with your attorney if you are not sure.

Don't expect the visits to go smoothly. They will be difficult. Adjusting to each other will take some time, and you will need to be patient and understanding. Tell your child about his or her room and sleeping arrangements in advance. Ask older children and teens for input about what they would like to do. Send them travel guides or links to websites with information about your area.

Prepare your child well in advance. If he or she has not been to your home, send photographs of your home and of the city or general area. Talk to your child about where you live and describe the places you will go and the things you will do together.

Don't forget that you can always come to your child's town and spend time with him or her there if the other parent agrees. This way, the child remains in a comfortable locale and may adjust to your presence better. Some parents like to travel to the child for pickup and then bring the child to their home. This way the visit starts in familiar surroundings and the child does not need to travel alone. You may also wish to travel someplace else with your child. Visiting a location close to his or her home may be a good solution if you live far away and are traveling by car.

Ways to Stay in Touch

Long-distance parenting is now easier than it ever has been because of the wealth of technology that is available. Consider using some of these methods to stay in touch.

Calls

Get the best long-distance calling plan you can and speak to your child on the phone several times a week if possible. Be sure to call on special occasions and holidays. If you are having trouble with the expense of these calls, try using one of the online calling services that allow you to essentially make a phone call from your computer to your child's computer over the Internet. Or buy your child calling cards so he or she can call you. For teens, you could also purchase cell phones with unlimited long-distance plans. Don't be hurt if your child does not want to spend a lot of time on the phone with you or gives short answers to your questions. It is important to make the effort of calling and letting your child hear your voice. Do not plan calls when they will be disruptive—at meal times, right before school, etc.

Mail

Send your child cards, letters, postcards, and brief notes so that he or she knows you are thinking of him or her. Children also appreciate receiving small, inexpensive gifts in the mail. If you cannot be together near holidays or your child's birthday, be sure to send a gift or card if you are able.

Videos

Use a home video recorder to create DVDs to send to your child by mail or online. Use video to show your child your home, your city, your office, and so on. Ask the other parent to send you DVDs or video files, or buy an older child a camera and ask him or her to use it to send you video.

Audio Tapes

Purchase a small, handheld microcassette recorder. Carry it with you and record short messages whenever you are thinking of your child. Purchase a recorder for your child to play your tapes on and to record messages to send back to you.

Web Cams

Purchase a web cam for your computer and your child's computer. You and your child can log on at the same time and communicate in real time and see each other while you are talking. (For more information about this, see the resources in Appendices B and C.)

Websites
You can set up a website for your child where homework, artwork, photos, and music can be posted for you to see. You can also create a page where you post things you want your child to see. Websites can be easily created using software that guides you through the process step by step. Websites such as **www.angelfire.com** allow you to set up a site for free using templates they provide. They host the site at no charge, but do run ads on the site.

Interactive Games
Some software programs allow you to play the game with another person over the Internet. One good example is Jumpstart Baby (from The Learning Company). The software is located at the child's home and a CD is sent to you. Using the software, you can play a computer game together over the Internet.

Email
Set up free email accounts for you and your child. Try **www.yahoo.com** or **www.hotmail.com**. You can then send messages as often as you wish at no charge, other than the cost of Internet access. If you don't have Internet access or a computer, you can use computers at your local library for no charge.

Instant Messenger
This is similar to email, but allows you and your child to send messages back and forth immediately. You can log on to the program when you are online and it will notify you when your child is also online and logged in. You then type messages back and forth that appear in a special box on your computer screen. You can download free instant messenger programs at **www.aol.com** or **www.msn.com**. You can also arrange specific times to chat through the program. You can also go into a private chat room and type instant messages to each other there.

Fax

If your home or office and the other parent's home have fax machines, you can fax notes, letters, drawings, cartoons you clipped, etc., to your child.

How you maintain contact with your child is unimportant. Maintaining some kind of regular contact is what is important.

LONG-DISTANCE PARENTING TIPS

➤ Have regular contact with your child—at least two times per week—if possible.

➤ Remember that whoever is moving has a lot to adjust to.

➤ Use a variety of methods to maintain contact, to make it fun, and to ease the cost of those expensive long-distance calls.

➤ Become familiar with new technology so you can use it to help stay in touch.

➤ Remember to give your child a variety of ways he or she can contact you as well.

➤ Keep your child involved in your life by sharing details about where you live, what you do, and where you go.

➤ Maintain contact with very young children, even if you are the one doing all the communicating.

➤ Plan in-person visits at least once a year.

➤ Remember that in-person visits may not be easy, but they are important.

➤ Try to share transportation expenses and responsibilities with the other parent, if possible.

➤ Send gifts and cards if you will not be together for holidays or your child's birthday.

11

OTHER PEOPLE INVOLVED WITH VISITATION

Divorce or separation is a very personal matter. Unfortunately, while going through the process, you probably realized that more people were involved in your personal matter than you ever dreamed possible. Now that you are through the process and are living with your parenting plan, you will find that you are not done with other people's involvement in your relationship with your child.

Teachers and Schools

It is essential that your child's school know about the divorce or separation and have your new contact information. You will need to call the school and explain that you need to receive separate notification of all school events, the school calendar, parent-teacher conference dates, and your child's report cards. More and more schools are attuned to these needs and have a process set up to allow for dual notification. If your child's school is uncooperative, first talk to the classroom teacher (or guidance counselor for middle and high school students) who may be able to facilitate what you need. If you still are not getting anywhere, you may need to provide the school with a copy of the section of your divorce judgment or custody order that states that you have access to these records. If you have nothing in writing about this, contact your attorney, who can assist you.

You will probably want to participate in school events and attend parent-teacher conferences. If your relationship with the other parent is on good terms, you can attend the same parent-teacher meetings. If not, it is not a problem to schedule a separate conference for you alone. Talk to the other parent to decide if you will sit together or separately at school events if you both attend.

You do need to remember that contact with your child's teacher is not an opportunity to complain about the other parent, blame things on the other parent, or pump the teacher for information about the other parent. The teacher can offer you insight as to how your child is adjusting to the change in home life and how it is impacting school performance. If your child consistently has problems the day after visitation, this is an indication that there are some adjustment issues that need to be dealt with. Take a look at the timing of the visits. Would it be easier for the child if he or she came home a bit earlier? Would the adjustment be better if you took the child to school instead of returning him or her to the other home the night before?

To help make things simpler in your dealings with the school, it may be a good idea to agree on some rules about which parent will be responsible for what. Many parents agree that the residential parent will handle all school paperwork. This does not always have to be the case, though. For example, it makes sense that the parent who will be with the child for the day in question be the one to sign a permission slip for a field trip or after-school event. If your child is going to be with you from Wednesday night to Saturday morning, and the school sends home a permission slip for a field trip that will happen on Friday, it may make sense for you to sign it. Of course, both parents need to know about it, in case of emergency or in case there is a change in the parenting schedule.

Additionally, children are sometimes required to get a signature from a parent on a test or report card. You can decide that one of you will always be responsible for this, or you can decide that whichever parent is with the child when he or she comes home from school with the item will be the one to sign it. Make sure the parent who is not signing has a chance to see the report card or test. Some parents decide that one parent will handle all paperwork for the sport the child plays and the other parent will handle all school paperwork. If you can have a standard plan in place for these kinds of things, you can prevent confusion.

Doctors and Dentists

You need to contact your child's doctor(s) and dentist to inform them about the divorce or separation. This is particularly important information for a pediatrician to have. Be sure to give your new contact information. If you are providing health insurance for your child and/or are the parent who is financially responsible for bills, be sure the office has current insurance information. Remember to give the other parent claim forms to take on appointments, if necessary, and make sure both you and the other parent have a health insurance card for your child. If you are not present for appointments, request that you receive a copy of the record from that appointment. It is also reasonable to ask that the doctor or dentist speak with you on the phone to provide an update on your child's health.

You may be asked to provide proof that you have a legal right to this information. If so, provide a copy of the portion of your divorce judgment or custody order giving you this right. Contact your attorney if you have nothing in writing. Talk to the other parent about alternating taking your child to the these appointments so you both have a chance to see the health care professionals.

If the other parent has sole custody, which means he or she has the sole authority to make important decisions about your child, this can mean that a doctor or hospital may not allow you to authorize medical care for your child. This can be a real problem if the other parent cannot be reached or is out of town. Discuss this problem with the other parent. Suggest that he or she could give you a written, notarized authorization to obtain medical care for your child when he or she is not available. You should keep a copy for yourself, give one to your child's pediatrician and dentist (and other doctors your child sees regularly), and one to the school. If you and the other parent have joint legal custody, with residence to the other parent and visitation to you, you do not need an authorization, since you already have the legal authority to make decisions about your child. You should point this out to your pediatrician and other health care workers to prevent any confusion.

AUTHORIZATION TO OBTAIN MEDICAL CARE

I, _____ am the mother/father of the child _____, whose date of birth is _____. I have sole custody of the child. I hereby authorize _____, the mother/father of the child, to make medical/dental/health decisions about the child and to authorize treatment for the child in my absence or if I cannot be reached.

_____
print name

_____   _____
sign name   date

Friends and Relatives

Now that you are divorced or separated, your family and friends are more important to you than ever. Your family and close friends are also an important part of your child's support system. While you want your child to continue to have contact with these people, you need to strike a balance. If you spend time with your child every other weekend, and take your child to your parents' home each of these weekends, you are sending a message that you do not want to be alone with your child. The other parent can also attempt to use this as a reason to limit your time. Involve your child with your family, but make sure you have time alone to develop your own relationship.

It is fine to have a friend drop over for a few hours while your child is with you. However, you are using your friends or family as a crutch if you need them with you all the time.

Former Relatives and Friends

Just as it is important for your child to have contact with your family and friends, he or she needs to remain in contact with the other parent's family and friends. You must refrain from making negative or derogatory comments about any of these people. Allow your child to talk about visits with these people, but do not press your child for details or be overly inquisitive. In short, it is none of your business.

Should you run into any of these people, be polite but distant. Do not get into a discussion about the divorce or separation, or about your child. The details of these things are for you and the other parent only. You do not need to justify or explain anything to your former relatives or former friends. Doing so will likely only result in bad feelings or conflict.

Dating

If you have someone new in your life that is or could be important to you, you need to do some evaluating before involving that person with your child. If you are at a point where you are casually dating different people, it is best not to seriously introduce them to and involve them with your child. It can be confusing. It is okay for you to date and for your child to know that you do, however. You are supposed to go on living!

If you have one person you are seeing regularly, you need to decide how serious you are or think you could be about the new relationship. If you think this person is important to you, it is fine to introduce him or her to your child. You should never present the new person as a replacement for the other parent and it is very important that you continue to have time alone with your child. Children and teens will be curious about this relationship and may ask if you plan on remarrying. It's best to be honest, but don't go in to the details about your relationship. You should also expect your child to exhibit some resentment, coldness, or rudeness towards this person. The only way to deal with this is with patience. Out-right rudeness or hostility should not be tolerated though, just as you would not tolerate it towards anyone else.

You will need to make your own personal and moral judgment about a new partner spending the night with you when your child is present. Whatever your choice, it is never appropriate for a child to witness overt adult sexual behavior.

DATING TIPS

- Date if you feel it is something you want to do.
- Do not get your child involved with all of the different people you date if you are playing the field.
- Be honest with your child about the fact that you are dating.
- Expect your child to have mixed emotions about you dating.
- Introduce your child to someone that is special with whom you are having (or hoping to have) a long-term relationship.
- Decide if you feel sleepovers with dates are appropriate when your child is at your home.
- Never make your child feel as if your new partner is somehow a replacement for the other parent, and do not place the new partner in a parental role.
- Do not let your dating life fill all of your free time with your child.
- Do not expect your child to be thrilled you are dating, or accept a new partner quickly.
- Never allow your child to witness inappropriate adult sexual activity.
- Do not make your new partner a part of the family too quickly.
- Do not discuss your dating life with the other parent or expect him or her to discuss his or hers with you.
- Do not get your child involved in your emotional roller coaster. He or she is not a confidant or pal. Keep any romantic angst to yourself.
- Remember that while you are supposed to have an adult social life, you want your child to feel cared for and important in your life.

Remarriage

Should you reach the point where you are going to remarry, you need to set some ground rules. The new spouse should never be referred to as "Mom" or "Dad" or whatever name the child uses for the other parent. The new spouse can have authority over the child since they will be sharing the same house, but you as the parent should be the one making all the important decisions about the child. If there are stepsiblings, you need your child to know he or she is not being replaced. The same goes for any half siblings that are later born into the family. There are resources listed in the appendix that can help you with these adjustments.

When the Other Parent Dates

If the other parent is dating, you should not be involved. It may be difficult, and you may feel hurt and betrayed, but you have to stay out of it. If your child talks about the person the other parent is dating, it is fine to listen, but don't make snide comments, ask a lot of questions, or in any way get involved. If the other parent begins dating one person seriously, you will certainly hear more about it. Don't believe everything your child says. If you run into the person, be civil and polite.

If your child is witnessing inappropriate adult sexual activity at the other parent's home, your first step should be (as always) to talk to the other parent. You can't believe everything your child is telling you. Express your concerns to the other parent. If you still believe that this is occurring or your child continues to tell you about other instances, then you need to talk to your attorney. Another option is to contact your local department of social or human services or state child abuse hotline. (see Appendices B and C.)

If the Other Parent Remarries

Should the other parent remarry, you can expect your child to be excited, happy, depressed, nervous, left out, angry, jealous, and so on. Your child will need reassurance that he or she will always be an important person to both you and the other parent. Remember that no stepparent can ever take your place or fill your shoes. It is not acceptable for the new stepparent to be called the same name as your child calls you ("Mom," "Daddy," "Ma," "Father," etc.), and if this is happening, you should have a polite and calm conversation with your child's other parent to express how you feel. If your child is the one initiating this, tell him or her how important your relationship is and explain that it hurts your feelings that this is happening. Ultimately, the other parent will be the one who will have to resolve this issue since it is happening in his or her home. Adjusting to a new stepparent will take time and you need to be patient with your child while this is happening.

Dealing with Stepfamily Problems

If you or the other parent remarries, your child is going to have to learn to live in a stepfamily. If you both remarry, your child will be in two stepfamilies. Living in a stepfamily can be a balancing act for all involved, particularly if there are stepchildren or half siblings in the family. If there are problems at the other parent's home, you can let the other parent know if your child is upset, but generally you need to stay out of it—unless you believe your child is emotionally or physically in danger.

If problems develop in your own stepfamily, try to deal with them with patience and understanding. Living in a stepfamily is not easy for children and there can be lots of issues. Join a local stepfamily support group, read some of the books recommended in Appendix B or visit some of the websites listed in that appendix. Get some support and don't be afraid to get some help from a counselor who specializes in stepfamily issues. Adjusting to a stepparent can be just as difficult as adjusting to divorce.

TIPS FOR STEPFAMILY PARENTING

➤ Do not expect your child to be thrilled about your remarriage.

➤ Explain to your child that the new spouse is not a replacement for the other parent.

➤ Help your child get to know stepsiblings before a marriage.

➤ Expect conflict in your stepfamily.

➤ Do not ask or allow your child to call the new stepparent by the same name he or she calls the other parent, or you.

➤ Make sure your child knows that he or she is an important part of the new family.

➤ Help the new spouse develop a relationship with your child. Do not expect them to have a parent-child relationship—the relationship cannot immediately take on this form. Eventually, your child may come to see the stepparent as a third parent.

➤ Allow your spouse to have reasonable authority over your child, but make sure everyone in the family remembers that YOU are the child's parent.

➤ Take the time to listen to your child's feelings and thoughts about the new marriage. Make sure that it is a priority in your family.

➤ If the new spouse has children, try to rearrange scheduling so that all of the children can be together sometimes. They will never develop good relationships if they do not see each other.

➤ Take the time to make your new marriage as successful as possible. Another divorce isn't going to be good for anyone.

➤ Get support from a stepfamily association or a counselor experienced in stepfamily issues if necessary.

➤ Make sure your child is an involved, active, and important member of your new family.

12

DEALING WITH AGES AND STAGES

Your child is constantly growing and changing, so it is unrealistic to expect that a parenting plan can be set in stone throughout his or her life. The plan is going to need to change as your child does. You can make changes simply by talking to the other parent and agreeing on them, you can meet with a mediator who will help you reach an agreement or you can speak to your attorneys and have them reach a settlement, or you can return to court and have the judge decide for you. It's always important to consider your child's current needs when making changes to your schedule.

This chapter will talk about the different needs children have and will give you some ideas as to how to modify your plan as they grow. Come back to this chapter for help as your child grows or when you or your child start to feel as if the visitation plan needs some changes.

Babies

If you have an infant, your parenting plan may allow for you to have frequent short visits or a traditional kind of schedule where you have the child for weekends. Generally, short frequent visits work best for infants, so if you have a traditional (every other weekend) plan and you find the child is having difficulty with it, try switching to the other type. Infants may display more frequent crying and problems with eating and digestion when they are disturbed or upset.

One complication to a parenting plan is with a breastfeeding infant. If the other parent is the mother and she is breastfeeding, then you will have difficulty keeping the child for long periods. Talk to the mother about the possibility of her pumping and freezing some breast milk so you can feed the baby from a bottle, and thus be able to take the child to your home or to visit your relatives. Be aware that breastfeeding can be a very emotional issue. Since pediatricians do recommend that children be breastfed for at least one year, you should try to encourage it and be supportive even if this means some inconvenience for you. Do not feed the baby formula if the mother is breastfeeding, unless it is something you talk about together and agree upon. Remember that this is something that will benefit the child—breastfeeding has proven beneficial impacts on health and intelligence.

If you are the mother and are trying to breastfeed during your visitation time, speak to a lactation specialist (your child's pediatrician may have one on staff or can provide a referral). It isn't impossible and it can be done.

Sleep issues are always a problem with an infant. You and the other parent need to try to work together to develop a plan. Are you going to try to get the child on a schedule at night and for naps or are you going to let the child decide when sleeping happens? It's important to be consistent and work cooperatively on this. If the other parent is trying to get the child to follow a specific schedule and you don't do the same thing, you're going to have a cranky child.

You and the other parent need to work together when solid foods are introduced and need to follow the same schedule for meals. Follow a set schedule for introducing new foods—you want to introduce one new food at a time so that if there are any food allergies they can be easily identified. Your pediatrician can provide more information about this.

Get some basic baby equipment to keep at your home so everything does not need to be transported each time. You can purchase a portable crib instead of a large, full-size one and a portable high-chair seat that straps onto a chair instead of a large, floor highchair. It can be helpful to send a written schedule back and forth that you will each fill in so you will know when the baby last ate and slept. (see Chapter 7.)

Toddlers

Toddlers are going through many changes and it is best to try to stick to a really tight schedule. Don't monkey around with it if you can help it.

A toddler will experience separation anxiety and have trouble separating from whichever parent they are with. Deal with separation anxiety by taking a little more time with transitions and making them more gradual. Toddlers also start to display aggression by biting, throwing, or hitting. Deal with this by consistently saying no and removing your child from the situation or item.

When your child is a toddler, he or she may be ready to begin spending the night at your home. Usually one night a week is good way to start, so you don't go two weeks between sleepovers. You want to get him or her used to this new event and grow accustomed to sleeping at your home. Toddlers may experience sleep disturbances, especially if they are adjusting to sleeping overnight at your home for the first time. Talk to the other parent about what works to comfort the child in the night. Stay calm and remember that toddlers scream and cry a lot and it isn't your fault!

Talk with the other parent about things like potty training, discipline, and sleeping schedules. Consistency really is important. Read up on toddler behavior and what to expect in this stage. Remember that toddlers are all about pushing the limits, and your child will want to find out what your limits are.

Make sure you have your home childproofed so your toddler cannot reach dangerous things, fall down stairs, or find small objects to put in his or her mouth.

Tantrums are going to be a fact of life, and you simply need to learn how to cope with them. A tantrum does not mean you should change your visitation plan. Tantrums are a normal part of your child's development and you need to develop the skills needed to manage them.

Preschoolers

When your child reaches the preschool age, you'll probably find that he or she is becoming more verbal and cognitive. He or she will probably ask you questions that go to the very root of things, such as, "Why do you live here and Mom lives at another house?" Give brief and honest answers to these kinds of questions. A good answer is, "Because some moms and dads don't live together."

Preschoolers can begin to handle a typical parenting plan, such as every other weekend at your home. If you do change to this kind of schedule, do so gradually and try to make sure you do continue to have some kind of weekly in-person contact with your child. This is why many parents see their children one weekday evening each week. Maintain phone contact with your child when you are not together. Some days he or she may want to talk for a long time and other days a brief hello will be all you get.

Preschoolers are ready to go places with you and do new and fun things. Consider joining a play group, or going to a single parent and child group get-together as an activity.

School-Age Children

When your child begins school, you may need to make some adjustments to your schedule. It's important to make sure your child gets enough sleep on school nights. You may want to spend most of your time together on weekends now. Regular, in-person contact during the week is important though, so consider working out a schedule where you have dinner or spend some after-school time with your child one weekday each week. Keep in contact with the other parent and your child's teacher about how things are going, and be prepared to make changes if it seems that the schedule is impacting the child's school behavior. Finding the right schedule can take some trial and error.

Your elementary-age child will ask you even more probing questions about the divorce or separation and the reasons for it. Answer questions honestly, but do not give details or deeply personal information unless it truly is helpful and will not cause the child to see the other parent in a bad light. Children of this age often display their emotions about your family through physical symptoms, like headaches and stomachaches. Try to keep your child comfortable, and always see a doctor if you believe he or she is truly ill. Be supportive and loving, yet firm about the schedule.

You need to begin to give consideration to your child's homework at this age. Elementary students now have more homework than you ever did. Make sure that your child has time to get homework done when he or she is at your home. Be available to answer questions and help out with problems. Let your child know that you would be happy to help him or her with a school project. This may mean that you will have to see your child at unscheduled times for trips to the library or to buy materials at a craft store. Talk to the other parent and get his or her support. Being involved in your child's life in this way can benefit everyone. Elementary children also have after-school activities and sports to consider.

Friends are becoming important at this age as well. Get to know your child's friends. Suggest that he or she invite a friend over to your home for the afternoon sometime when the child is with you. A sleepover might also be something to suggest once a year, but not something you will want to do on a regular basis since your time together is limited. Expect that your child may want to go to a friend's home during your scheduled time. Allowing this to happen occasionally will show that his or her friendships are important to you. A parenting plan is not a prison sentence that prohibits other normal and fun activities.

Attend your child's sports events, concerts, and performances. These do not have to fall onto a regularly scheduled visitation day for you to go. You might want to let the other parent know you intend to go so that there is not a scene when he or she is surprised by your presence.

Preteens

Kids in the eight to twelve year age range are often called *tweens* since they are in a stage between early childhood and the teen years. Tweens act a lot like teens sometimes. They are interested in popular culture, fashion, music, movies, and trends, but they are still children in many ways. Just because your tween listens to the hottest new music and is sporting a new hairstyle does not mean that he or she doesn't want or need your love, attention, and time.

Tweens sometimes try very hard to be perfect in the hopes that this will bring their parents back together. Make sure your child knows no one is perfect and nothing can bring you and the other parent back together. Tweens also often begin to take sides or assign blame for the divorce or separation (to the parents or themselves). Explain to your child that he or she is not to blame and also that there are two people in a marriage or relationship, and both in some way cause a breakup.

Your child will have even more homework now, lots of friends, and activities. It's important that you continue to follow a schedule and make sure that time for you is built into the child's life. Let your child be active and busy, find a way for you to be involved in his or her interests, and make sure you continue to have time to spend together.

The Teen Years

You remember being a teenager. Nothing about it was easy. It's even harder today, especially when you have parents who live in separate houses making different and sometimes competing demands on you.

Your teen deals with the divorce or separation in a way different from younger children. He or she does continue to have feelings of loss, grief, anger, and sadness, but also blames him- or herself for the situation. Teens also often feel that they will never be able to have a stable relationship and should avoid marriage. It's important to talk about these feelings with your child and help him or her understand that no blame falls on his or her shoulders, and that many marriages do work out.

Teens often feel they have had to grow up too quickly because of the divorce or separation. There isn't much you can do about this, other than to insulate him or her from disputes between you and the other parent, and avoid confiding in him or her like a friend. Teens frequently worry about money, and feel involved in child support and even alimony. Don't involve your teen in child support or alimony matters. Teens do need to start to understand finances and budgets, but you should not unload your financial worries on your teen. Additionally, teens feel a need to take on adult responsibility, and fill the gaps at both homes. Remember, your teen is not an adult and is not a substitute for the other parent, and should not be expected to fill his or her role.

Your teen will need to be consulted about the schedule. Independence is important at this age. Teens not only have a lot of homework and afterschool activities, but friends are now the most important thing in his or her world. Many teens also have jobs. Working out a schedule may be difficult. It's going to require some compromise on all fronts. Your teen is working hard at becoming an adult, and he or she must learn that compromise is an important skill.

Dating is another conflict with parenting plans. What teen is going to give up a date with the guy or girl of his or dreams to hang out with Mom or Dad? None. You've got to somehow reach a balance. If your teen spends every weekend day and evening dating, you'll never see each other. Talk to your teen and tell him or her you don't want to mess up his or her social life. Suggest you reserve maybe one weekend a month or two Sundays a month to spend just with each other. At your other scheduled times, the teen can date and you will spend time together before and after dates, parties, get-togethers and so on. Your teen needs to know that you support his or her lifestyle, but also that you want to make your relationship a priority.

Expect to be met with resistance, outbursts, attitudes, refusals to communicate—all those things you may have done to your own parents. You will need to make changes in the schedule to accommodate your teen's life, but there does need to be some kind of regular time together. Many parents find that they are comfortable without a schedule. They let their teen drop in or stay the night whenever the mood strikes. If this works for you and the other parent, then go ahead and do it. Other parents feel that they need to have a schedule to follow so they can organize their own lives. You'll have to work out what works best for your family.

If you have a plan that your teen refuses to follow no matter what you do, you need to take a look at it and determine what the problem is. Does he or she resent being away from friends? Can you make any changes or allowances that will make the plan easier to live with? Do you need to make some scheduling changes? Involve your teen in this process and demonstrate that you are willing to be flexible while still maintaining a strong commitment to your relationship.

Unfortunately, there are teens who decide they do not want to live under a parenting plan and do not want to spend time with you. If your teen absolutely refuses to cooperate, and nothing you and the other parent say or do makes a difference, then you might find you have to back off for a while. Let him or her skip some planned time with you. Give a little break and then come back and try again. The important thing is to try again. Don't give up and walk away. Your child really does need to see that you care and that you won't give up. If you and the other parent keep trying and your child refuses to cooperate, unfortunately, there isn't much you can do. Courts pay attention to what teens say they want when it comes to visitation. You can't force a sixteen-year-old to come, but you can refuse to give up and continue to show that you care and that you are available for him or her.

When Your Child is Grown

Once your child is over age eighteen, he or she is not subject to the parenting plan any longer. This doesn't mean that your work is done! You will want to continue to maintain regular contact with your child and continue to do things together and be a family. If your child goes away to college, you'll have less opportunity for in-person contact, but you can still maintain phone and email contact. College kids and young adults still need parents. Make yourself available to him or her and continue to give advice, show interest in what he or she is doing, and be a part of his or her life.

It is hard to learn to let go and let your child become independent, and watch him or her do things that you may see as mistakes. You and the other parent did the best job you could, and your child really will be fine. Pat yourself on the back for creating and raising such a good person.

Brothers and Sisters

This book has talked about "your child" in a singular sense. Many parents have more than one child. When you have two or more children, you will have to cope with their conflicting schedules, conflicting abilities, and of course, with their conflicts, period.

You'll want to try to keep to a schedule that will allow you to see your children at the same time when they are both available. You are a family unit and it is important to spend time together. Things are going to come up, however. Your daughter might have a basketball game one weekend and your son might have play rehearsal another. Follow your parenting schedule and take your kids to their planned events. Spend time with them all together when possible, and enjoy the individual time you will have with them as well. If you lived together every day, that's what you would do. Fit in your family time around the events.

If you have children far apart in age, it is always difficult to find activities that they all can do and enjoy. Just do your best. You might have to do some multi-tasking—playing dinosaurs on the floor with a four-year-old while bouncing a five-month-old and helping an eight-year-old do homework. And, of course, your kids are going to grow and change and this will change what they are interested in and capable of. Things are always changing in a family. Spending time together as a family is what's important. Go through the suggested activities in Chapter 7 and try different things. You can't keep everybody happy all of the time, but you can vary your activities so that everyone gets to do something he or she enjoys at some point.

Brothers and sisters fight. This is just a rule of the universe. Your kids don't fight because you got divorced or separated. They just fight because that is what siblings do. Set limits, create rules, and always make sure no one is physically harmed. Read some parenting books about coping with siblings. Talk to friends and family for suggestions about how to handle it. Discuss possible solutions with the other parent. Make it clear that everyone must follow certain rules in your home.

There will be a time when your children are certain you are playing favorites. Often, kids have difficulty understanding that children of different ages need different care, supervision, and inter-action. Parent as you see fit and reassure them that you love each child equally but in a unique way. Talking with the other parent will allow you to coordinate efforts, share insights, and work together with your children.

13

SPECIAL SITUATIONS

Each family is unique and no one experiences the exact same set of problems. This chapter will help you work through some specific problems that may be unique to your family.

Physical or Sexual Abuse

If you child has been, or you honestly believe he or she may have been, physically or sexually abused by the other parent (or by anyone else for that matter), you must first obtain whatever emergency medical care is needed. You need to contact your state's social services department or the police to report the abuse. (Child abuse hotline numbers are listed in Appendix D.) You then will need to cooperate with the caseworkers who investigate the report. Obtain counseling for your child to assist with the mental and emotional damage that has been done. Contact your attorney to find out if you should seek sole custody.

Substance Abuse

If you have a problem with substance abuse, the most important thing is to get treatment. If you are dealing with this, and your child is old enough to understand, tell him or her about your problem, what you are doing about it, and the mistakes you made that got you here. If you feel the other parent has developed a substance abuse problem, you need to talk to your attorney and call the child abuse hotline, since this constitutes neglect. If you suspect or know that your child is using drugs, it is imperative that you get him or her help immediately. There are some organizations and information clearinghouses listed in Appendix B that can help you with this. You need to speak with the other parent immediately. Get a referral to a treatment center or substance abuse counselor from your child's pediatrician. You can contact law enforcement—but this should only be a last resort.

Mental Illness

It is normal for your child to react to the divorce or separation and resulting adjustment with anger, depression, fear, regression (acting younger than the child is), sadness, guilt, and so on. For some children, these reactions might be quite severe. There is a fine line between a normal reaction to the divorce and an abnormal reaction. If your child endangers him- or herself or threatens to harm him- or herself, you need to get mental health assistance immediately. If your child's attitude and emotions seem to be making it impossible for him or her to live a normal life, you need to get help.

You know your child. If you feel that his or her reaction is just not right, get help. First it is imperative to talk to the other parent. You can handle the best if you both work together. If there is any question in your mind as to whether or not your child would benefit from mental health assistance, then you should err on the side of caution and get help. Your child's pediatrician can make a referral to a counselor or therapist. A child who does not need therapy will be identified by the therapist, so you won't do any harm by taking your child to a therapist. Chapter 2 contains a list of the common symptoms of depression.

SIGNS YOU MAY NEED TO GET HELP FOR YOUR CHILD

➤ He or she is extremely detached and displays very little emotion or reaction to anything.

➤ He or she talks about suicide or harming him- or herself, or actually attempts self-harm.

➤ He or she is frequently violent and destructive.

➤ He or she is withdrawn, sad, and depressed.

➤ He or she is overly nervous, obsessive, or compulsive.

➤ He or she cries far more than is normal for the age.

➤ He or she is constantly hostile to you or the other parent.

➤ He or she is experiencing serious difficulty at school (and this is a new problem).

➤ He or she has regressed substantially and has remained so for a long time.

Note: These are some general warning signs. Only a trained mental health worker can know if your child needs treatment. These descriptions are basic and are not determinative. It is normal for a child to display some of these signs (but self-harm is never normal) in a mild way when coping with divorce, separation, and visitation. You should be concerned if you see these symptoms on a long-term consistent basis. If you are ever in doubt, seek assistance from a mental health worker.

If you feel that you are experiencing depression, anxiety, or other mental health problems, seek help. There are many treatments available and it is important to recognize that these are illnesses, just like pneumonia or asthma. Don't worry about what other people think. You cannot be an adequate parent if your own problems go untreated.

If the other parent exhibits signs of mental illness, you need to contact your attorney. Family and friends may be able to support your suspicions about this. Do not involve your child! If you feel he or she is unsafe at home, contact the child abuse hotline for your area and speak to your attorney.

Reservations about the Other Parent

Almost all divorced parents, at some time or another, have reservations about the other parent's parenting abilities. If you're honest with yourself, you've probably had doubts about your own parenting abilities at some point! Just because you do not agree with the decisions or actions of the other parent does not mean that he or she is an unfit parent. It is helpful to remember that at some point, you did believe he or she was a good parent, otherwise you would not have chosen to have a child with him or her.

There are people who are simply terrible parents. If the other parent is part of this group, you need to ask yourself why you did not act on it during the divorce. Why didn't you make sure the judge knew? If nothing has changed between then and now, perhaps you are just feeling very angry, hurt, or depressed. If you believed this was true, why didn't you take steps to protect your child then?

There are certainly instances in which people have drastically changed after a divorce or separation. Some people even develop mental illnesses after a divorce or separation. If this has happened with the other parent, you should contact your attorney to discuss your options, which may include returning to court to seek a change in custody. It is also very important that you document everything you can—keep a log or diary of the incidents that have concerned you, obtain copies of all medical or school records that will support your case. Do not involve your child at this stage. If you do return to court or mediation, you will need to tell your child this is happening and provide a brief explanation (such as "Mom/Dad and I are having some differences of opinion about where you should spend your time, and we are asking the judge to help us").

If the other parent was a terrible parent before the divorce or separation, and you did all you could to let the court know and you still lost, there isn't much you can do. You will have to be on the lookout for examples that support your opinion and keep track of them so that you can ask for a change of custody in the future.

While necessary in some situations, this kind of approach will ensure that your relationship with the other parent continues to be difficult and will impact your child. What is best for your child is for you to avoid conflict with the other parent when possible. Unless you honestly feel your child is in danger or is extremely miserable when with the other parent, try to just get on with things and accept your situation.

Moving

If you or your child is moving away from one another, read Chapter 10 about long-distance parenting. If the other parent is moving out of the area, you should consult your attorney because he or she may not be able to do so without court approval. There are limits on relocation by residential or residential parents. You want to make sure that even if the relocation is permitted that you will continue to be able to have regular contact with your child.

Changing Your Mind

After living as a nonresidential parent for a while, you may have come to the conclusion that the arrangement is not working for you or your child. If you decide you want more time with your child or would like custody, think about whether this is really what would be best for your child or if it is something you want. Many nonresidential parents begin to feel like a lesser parent after getting into the parenting schedule. If this is the case, get more involved with your child. Go to his or her dance classes, cub scout meetings, sports events, and so on. Suggest to the other parent that the child be with you instead of a sitter when he or she goes out. Look at what you can do, and how you and the other parent can compromise and work together to improve the situation without involving the courts. If none of this is possible or it doesn't solve the underlying problem, contact your attorney.

Getting your attorney involved will often mean a return to court, which will have an effect on your child. Children are made aware of court proceedings simply because it is almost impossible to hide it from them. Also, your child may be assigned a law guardian or guardian ad litem who will represent your child in court. This attorney will need to meet with and speak to your child. It is always best to try to work something out on your own without a return to court. If you and the other parent just can't find a compromise, try using a mediator. Your child need not be involved in the way he or she is in a formal court proceeding.

If You Want to Wash Your Hands of the Situation

Some nonresidential parents feel overwhelmed and frustrated with the demands of their parenting plan. They are tired of dealing with the other parent, tired of trading the child back and forth, and just want out. You can never be out. This is your child and even if you walk away, you are still an important figure in his or her life and will always be. You can't change that. If you are feeling like you no longer wish to deal with the demands of the parenting plan, look at what exactly about it is bothering you. Are you not getting enough sleep? Is your schedule too crowded? Is the other parent being unpleasant to you? Are you having too many conflicts with the other parent? Are you and your child having conflicts? Are there other things wrong in your life? Could you reduce visitation for a while to give yourself a break?

Try to get at the root of the problem and see if you can fix that first. If you don't see what you can change, try seeing a therapist. He or she may be able to help you change things to make them easier to cope with. Whatever you do, do not give up. When you created this child, you gave a lifetime commitment to always do your best to love and care for him or her. This cannot be broken. Don't disappear from your child's life, no matter how frustrated, tired, or overwhelmed you are.

Coping with Supervised Visitation

Some nonresidential parents are only permitted to have supervised visitation with their children. This means that another adult who is approved by the court must be present during parenting time. If you have supervised visitation, the first thing to do is to stop being angry about it. Of course, it is insulting to be watched when you are with your own child, whether there is a legitimate reason for it or not.

If you are living with supervised visitation, your goal should be to focus on your child during the times you are together. Pretend the supervising person is not in the room and spend some quality time with your child, playing, talking, singing, reading, or just goofing around. Bring some things with you to do during visitation if the facility doesn't have a lot of toys or games. Do not complain to your child about the situation. Put a smile on your face and concentrate on sharing some joy with your child. Treat it not as a prison sentence, but as precious parenting time.

If you believe that you should have unsupervised visitation, you need to talk to your attorney. The best way to convince a court to give you unsupervised visitation is to attend each and every supervised visitation, be pleasant and polite to the supervisor, and show appropriate behavior towards your child. It may also be helpful for you to take a parenting class. These classes will help you improve your parenting skills and will also show the court that you are trying to be a good parent. Seeing a therapist is also often looked upon favorably by the courts. If domestic violence or abuse is the reason given for why you must have supervised visitation, join a support group or seek treatment available for abusers. Even if these accusations against you are false, the court obviously believed them. Doing these things will make the court happy and will greatly increase your chances of doing away with the supervised visitation.

If you have a problem with the person who is supervising the visitation or the location where it is taking place, try to come up with some alternatives and contact your attorney about them.

Homosexuality

Sometimes a marriage or relationship ends because one of the partners realizes he or she is homosexual. Other times, a discovery such as this happens or comes to light after the divorce or separation. If you are the parent who has made this discovery, it is your choice as to how open you would like to be about it with your child. Certainly your child's age should play an important part in how much you choose to discuss. It is wise to make sure the other parent is aware of your sexual orientation first. It is also a good idea to let him or her know you are going to discuss it with the child so he or she is not blindsided. When introducing your child to same sex dates and partners, you should follow the same guidelines included in Chapter 11 for dating.

If the other parent is homosexual, you need to deal with your own feelings about the revelation. It is important that you not make any negative or derogatory remarks to your child about this. Also, it should be up to the other parent if he or she would like to let the child know about his or her sexual orientation. Your role will be to support the child and provide support after the information is shared. It is important for you to understand that courts do not believe a person's sexual orientation affects his or her parenting abilities.

Teens

If you are the parent of a teen, you know that everything is different for teens. You probably had to modify your house rules, your discipline style, and even your communication style when your child became a teen. Visitation is no exception. Teens handle divorce differently from children of any other age. While they experience the same feelings of loss, grief, anger, sadness, etc., they also take blame on themselves for the divorce. Many also see the divorce as proof that they will never have a stable relationship and that they should never get married. You will need to work through these feelings with your teen and help him or her realize that no one is to blame for the divorce and that it is not a prediction of the child's future relationships.

Teens need to be consulted about parenting plans and schedules. They are at a point in their lives where their friends are the most important thing in the world and they are also working very hard to be independent of their parents. While teens should have input, they should not be permitted to make the final decisions all the time.

As you begin to implement your parenting plan involving your teen, you will meet with resistance, outbursts, and even refusals to communicate. Your parenting plan is flexible, but it is not optional. Allowances can be made for your teen's schedule, job, and friends, but the bottom line is that the plan must be basically honored.

When Your Child Won't Visit

Children of all ages will sometimes refuse to go with you for your scheduled parenting time. Your position must be that the schedule is flexible, but it is not optional. You can and will make changes, but the basic schedule itself must be implemented. Children should have input into visitation, but should not make decisions.

What do you do if an eight-year-old refuses to come out the door? What if a five-year-old hides under the bed? First, assess the problem. Does the child resist the transition, but adjust once it is over? If so, think of ways you can ease the transition. See Chapter 7 for ideas about easing transition problems.

If nothing works, and your child still refuses to come with you, you must insist that he or she come. As a parent, you are often in the position of making your child do something he or she does not want. It's never fun and it's never pretty, but as a parent you must enforce your authority. Your child may be unconsciously testing you to see how serious you are about your parenting time. It's important that you and the other parent present a united front about this issue. Discuss it with the other parent to ensure cooperation. Even if he or she is enabling the child, you need to hold your ground. Speak to your attorney if the other parent is regularly canceling visitation.

A Child with Special Needs

If you have a child who has special needs, visitation is going to be even more challenging. It is important that you discuss the visitation plan with the child's doctor or therapist, and that you take their advice. Some children will need special equipment at each home, others are emotionally challenged and may have a difficult time with short visits. Your child's specialists can help you with many of these problems and situations.

If your child receives medication, it is wise to have the doctor write down the dosage schedule for you so there are no mix-ups. Be sure the medication is transported with the child.

Some nonresidential parents feel apprehensive about spending time with their special needs children. You don't need to feel this way. This is your child who loves you. You are his or her parent and cannot be replaced. Learn whatever you need to in order to care for your child and then enjoy your time together.

As with all children, visitation may be difficult sometimes, but it will be well worth the effort involved.

Parental Abduction

Parental abduction accounts for the majority of missing children. Should this ever happen in your family, you need to immediately contact the police with recent photos of your child and the other parent if possible. You need to obtain a copy of your judgment or order that gives you visitation rights, and provide this to the police. There are organizations listed in Appendices B and C that can assist you should this ever happen. It is also important for you to remember that you are legally authorized to be with your child during scheduled times and other times you and the parent have agreed to. If the other parent does not agree that you should have the child at an unscheduled time and you take the child anyhow, you may be guilty of parental abduction, or at the very least, a violation of your custody order.

Illness

If your child is ill when your time is scheduled, you should carefully consider your options. If the child has a high fever or has a gastrointestinal illness, it is probably best if you reschedule, because no one wants to be shuffled from house to house in that condition and he or she might be contagious. If the other parent must leave town or for some reason cannot care for the child, talk to the other parent about you going to stay with the child at his or her home. If this will not work, you will need to take the child with you and make him or her as comfortable as possible.

A child with a minor illness, such as a cold, is able to travel and go with you as planned. Keep your child as comfortable as possible, and remember that many children fondly remember the times a parent cared for them during illness.

Things that Supercede Visitation

There are situations that will essentially supercede your schedule:

♦ a seriously ill or hospitalized child;

♦ extreme weather conditions that prevent travel;

♦ family emergencies;

♦ a parent's serious illness; or,

♦ death of a family member.

If your child is quite ill, you will probably want to stop in to see him or her for a brief visit. Arrange this with the other parent. If the child is in the hospital, you can take turns visiting at different parts of the day.

If there is a weather emergency that makes it unsafe to travel, the child should stay where he or she is. You can resume your normal schedule after it is over. He or she should have phone contact (if possible) with the other parent.

If either you or the other parent is seriously ill, you will be unable to care for your child. The healthy parent can step in, and help can also be found from relatives and friends.

Should a family member pass away, your child, if he or she is old enough, will want to be able to be with that side of the family and attend gatherings and services. Make adjustments to the schedule to allow for this.

Other unexpected situations can arise, such a parent being delayed by a car accident or an emergency at work. You and the other parent should try to be flexible in these situations. The important thing is to make sure your child is not frightened by the unexpected change or delay.

For Those in the Military

If you are in the military, you may be away from your child for long periods of time. Read the chapter about long-distance visitation to learn some coping strategies. Make sure you explain to your child why you will be away. You and the other parent will need to cooperate so that you can have long periods of visitation when you are in the area, which will mean remaining flexible.

Traveling for Work

If you travel often for work, you may find it is difficult to follow a regular visitation schedule. Try to work with the other parent to arrange visitation for the times you are home. Read the chapter about long-distance visitation for tips on how to stay connected to your child while you are away.

An Adopted Child

If your child was adopted (either by both of you, or was the natural child of one of you and adopted by the other parent), you should follow the advice offered in this book. Simply because one or both you is not the child's biological parent should not alter or change anything. When the child was adopted, he or she legally became your child, with both of you as his or her parents. A divorce, separation, or end of relationship cannot change that. An adoption cannot be undone.

If your child knows that he or she was adopted (as most children do these days), he or she may feel as if the divorce or separation means that somehow the adoption will come undone as well. Reassure him or her that this cannot happen, and that both of you will continue to be parents in his or her life forever. For some teens, a divorce or separation can spur him or her to try to locate his or her biological parents. Should this issue come up, you should discuss it with your child and offer him or her support in whatever he or she decides to do. It is important to remember that if the biological parents are located, they cannot take your place in your child's life.

Shared Parenting

Some families have a 50/50 arrangement in their parenting plans, in which each parent spends about half the time with the children. These kinds of arrangements can be alternate weeks, alternate months, or any other kind of schedule that nets out as an equal split. This kind of arrangement is great because it means you each get equal time with your kids, but it can be difficult because the kids are always on the move.

Shared parenting can be wonderful, or it can be a complete disaster. You both get to be very involved in your children's lives on a day to day basis, but it can be a bit hectic and confusing at times and requires good cooperation between parents.

To make shared parenting successful, follow these suggestions.

♦ *Be a schedule freak.* Keep an accurate calendar and be clear about who is supposed to be where, and when.

♦ *Develop a smooth transition.* You're transferring your child back and forth on a regular basis, so you're going to need a solid transition plan. (See Chapter 7 for more information about transitions.)

♦ *Accept that the other parent is going to be a regular part of your life.* You're going to see a lot of each other, so it's a good idea to make some sort of peace with each other.

♦ *Try to be flexible.* Your agreement is to share your time with your children. If that means the other parent ends up with one extra day this week because of the way everyone's schedules fall, don't make a big deal out of it. Your goal should be that you end up with equal parenting times over a long period of time. Don't count the hours and get into a detailed accounting unless there are real problems with your arrangement.

Shared Residence

Some parents work out an arrangement where for a period of time (usually the first year or so after separation or divorce, as a transition phase), they maintain the marital residence as the children's home and each parent gets a separate apartment of their own. The parents then take turns living with the children in the marital home. For example, the mother would live at the home one week and the father would live there the next.

This kind of arrangement gives the children a sense of stability. They are still being parented in one home and they don't have to pack up and move around. It can be a gradual way of helping everyone adjust to the divorce. The downfalls of this are that it can be expensive (since your family is maintaining three residences instead of two) and you and your spouse are still sharing a living space, which can lead to conflict. To make this kind of situation work, follow these suggestions.

♦ *Create household rules.* Decide who is going to do what household chores. Not discussing these decisions is guaranteed to lead to conflict. You couldn't live together in harmony when you were married, so there is no reason to assume that you can easily do so now. Make compromises and try to come up with some rules you both can live by.

♦ *Be honest if it is not working.* This kind of arrangement might work well for your family for a few months, but you might find that you or your kids are growing out of it. If that happens, reassess your situation.

♦ *Make the kids part of your new lives.* It's too confusing to have one parent just disappear for a week or however long a shift is. Make sure your child sees where you're living and understand what you're doing. Maintain regular phone, email, or instant messenger contact while away.

14

CONCLUSION

Now that you've read this book, you know that there is no easy answer or quick fix to make your parenting plan easy and comfortable for everyone. Being the nonresidential parent is difficult, and the other parent has a row to hoe that's pretty tough too. You have lots of problems between you that can never be worked out and lots of emotions that pop up at the most inconvenient times. However, you are and always will be parents together. Your child is your common bond and this book was designed to help you use that to make visitation workable.

Many families get tripped up by problems with parenting schedules and end up constantly going back to court. That kind of life isn't good for anyone. This book has shown you the common pitfalls and ways to work around them and avoid them completely. Now that you've read the book, share it with the other parent. Then sit down together and try to follow some of the suggestions in the book. Keep this book on your bookcase and refer back to it as problems and situations come up in the coming years. Use Appendices B and C to get additional help from organizations, books, and websites.

It can be hard to live with a parenting schedule. It is difficult for you to work with the other parent to make sure that you are able to have time with your child at scheduled times and at other times when you might want it. Remember to keep yourself focused on your time with your child. Don't let disputes and problems with the other parent get in the way. Your relationship with your child is what is important. This book has shown you how to work with the other parent to keep your parenting plan a constant part of your life and your child's life. You can't change the other parent, but you can focus on your time with your child and make that your priority.

If you come away with nothing else, remember that your parenting plan is not about you or the other parent, but about your child and his or her needs. Making it work sometimes means gritting your teeth, compromising, and even sometimes just giving in. It will be worth it and your child will benefit from having two parents who work hard to make his or her life better.

Your situation will get easier as you live and work with it, and you will see your child adjust as well. The future is bright for both of you and your time with your child is an important part of that future.

Appendix A

SAMPLE PARENTING PLANS

SAMPLE 1

The following is an informal list of visitation rules developed by one couple.

- If you will be more than twenty minutes late picking up or dropping off, call and let the other parent know.
- Discussions about schedule changes are okay in front of the child, but arguments and heated discussions will be postponed until the child is not present.
- All of the child's laundry will be done at the residential parent's home.
- Schedule changes can be made at any time as long as we both agree. Each will notify the other parent of any changes as far in advance as possible.
- The child can call the parent he or she is away from at any time.
- The residential parent will share all school notices, report cards, etc., with the nonresidential parent.
- We will attend the same parent-teacher conferences, if they can be scheduled conveniently.
- School books, instruments, and sports equipment will travel with the child.
- We will try to use each other for babysitting, if possible.
- We will try to spend some time together as a family on Christmas Day and will alternate all other holidays.
- We will respect each other's judgment about bedtimes, curfews, and daily schedules.

SAMPLE 2

The following is a formal parenting plan developed by another couple.

We agree that our son, Trevor, shall reside with his mother, Kristin, and spend time with his father, Marcus. Marcus shall have time with Trevor as follows.

a) Every second weekend of the month, from school dismissal on Friday until school begins on Monday morning.

b) Every fourth weekend of the month on Saturday from 9:00 a.m. until 8:00 p.m.

c) Every Wednesday from school dismissal until 7:00 p.m.

d) In even-numbered years on the following holidays, from 10:00 a.m. until 9:00 p.m.: New Year's Day, Memorial Day, Labor Day, Thanksgiving, Christmas Eve, and the child's birthday.

e) In odd-numbered years on the following holidays from 10:00 a.m. until 9:00 p.m.: Easter, Fourth of July, Columbus Day, the day after Thanksgiving, Christmas Day, New Year's Eve.

f) Four days during winter school break and four days during spring school break, commencing at 10:00 a.m. on the first day and ending at 8:00 p.m. on the last day.

g) Every Father's Day and every year on Marcus's birthday.

h) If visitation is supposed to occur on Mother's Day or Kristin's birthday, that day in the schedule will be cancelled.

i) Two full weeks during summer vacation, which will not be scheduled to conflict with Kristin's family's reunion.

j) At other times as we both agree.

k) We will make the schedule together each year in January and adjust it as necessary if we both agree.

We agree that the following procedures will be followed.

1) Kristin shall be responsible for transporting Trevor to Marcus's home at the start of visitation, unless Marcus is scheduled to pick Trevor up at school that day.

2) Marcus shall be responsible for transporting Trevor to Kristin's home at the end of visitation, unless he is scheduled to return him directly to school.

3) Neither parent shall enter the other parent's home unless asked in.

4) Drop off times will have a ten minute leeway in either direction.

5) Trevor will bring clothing for the time he is with Marcus, and all clothing that is taken on visitation will be returned with Trevor.

6) All of Trevor's belongings that are taken on visitation will return with him.

7) Trevor will have access to the phone to call or answer a call from whichever parent he is away from at the time.

8) Changes to the visitation schedule must be requested at least 24 hours in advance, except in emergency situations.

9) Neither parent will drive Trevor in the car after consuming alcohol.

10) Trevor will not be taken to any bars during visitation.

11) If either parent takes Trevor on vacation, contact information will be given to the other parent.

The following rules will apply to Trevor's routine at both homes.

1) Bedtime is at 9:00 p.m., unless a special event or special occasion occurs.

2) Both parents will make sure Trevor is dressed appropriately before leaving the house.

3) Computer time is not to occur until after all homework is completed, and is limited to one hour per day.

4) Whichever parent is with Trevor at the time is expected to transport him to soccer practice and games.

Marcus has access to Trevor's school and medical records. The following rules will be followed.

1) Marcus is responsible for contacting the school and doctors to get copies of records, report cards, notices and calendars.

2) Marcus will schedule a separate parent-teacher conference if he wishes to attend one.

3) Marcus and Kristin may attend the same school events, concerts, sports games, and ceremonies, if their schedules allow.

Appendix B

RESOURCES

Live-Away Dads
by William C. Klattle

Mom's House, Dad's House: Making Two Homes for Your Child
by Isolina Ricci

No-Fight Divorce: Using Mediation to End Your Marriage with Less Conflict, Time, and Money
by Brette McWhorter Sember

Parenting Teenagers: Systematic Training for Effective Parenting of Teens
by Don Dinkmeyer, et al

Single Fatherhood: The Complete Guide
by Chuck Gregg

Single Mamahood: Advice and Wisdom for the African-American Single Mother
by Kelly Williams

The Single Parent Resource
by Brook Noel, Arthur C. Klein, Art Klein

Stepfamily Realities: How to Overcome Difficulties and Have a Happy Family
by Margaret Newman

Still a Dad: The Divorced Father's Journey
by Serge Prengel

Surviving the Breakup: How Children and Parents Cope With Divorce
by Judith S. Wallerstein

The Tween Years
by Donna G. Corwin

The Unexpected Legacy of Divorce: A 25 Year Landmark Study
by Judith Wallerstein

Vicki Lansky's Divorce Book for Parents: Helping Your Child Cope with Divorce and Its Aftermath
by Vicki Lansky

Wonderful Ways to be a Stepparent
by Judy Ford and Anna Chase

Your Baby and Child
by Penelope Leach

MAGAZINES FOR PARENTS

Dadmag newsletter
www.dadmag.com

Divorce Magazine
2255 B Queen St. East, Suite 1179
Toronto, ON M4E-1G3 Canada
416-368-8853
www.divorcemagazine.com

Fathering Magazine
www.Fathermag.com

WEBSITES FOR PARENTS

About.com Single Parents
http://singleparents.about.com

Air Force Family Separation and Readiness (tips for visitation for military families)
www.afcrossroads.com/amseparation/index.cfm

Breastfeeding and Visitation Plans
www.lalecheleague.com

Celebrating Children: Single African American Parenting
www.celebratingchildren.com

Discussion Board for Custodial Parents
www.mafiaboard.com/forum

Divorce Interactive
www.divorceinteractive.com

Fathers are Parents, Too
www.fapt.org

Fathers Network
www.fathersnetwork.org

**Making Lemonade:
Single Parent Network**
www.makinglemonade.com

**National Organization
of Single Mothers**
www.singlemothers.org

Relocation
www.thelizlibrary.org/lamusga/
glenn.html
www.apa.org/releases/relocation
.html

Responsible Single Fathers
www.singlefather.org

Sample Visitation Plans
www.familymediationcouncil.com/
publicreading.htm

Single Mothers on Mission
www.singlemoms.org

Single Parent Central
www.singleparentcentral.com/
index.htm

Single Parent Tips
www.singleparent-tips.com/
OurGurus.asp

Single Parents Network
www.singleparentsnetwork.com

Single Parents World
www.parentsworld.com

**Single Rose Resource
for Single Mothers**
www.singlerose.com

**The International Stepfamily
Foundation**
www.istepfamily.com

Woman's Divorce
www.womansdivorce.com

ORGANIZATIONS FOR PARENTS

**African American Family Services
(AAFS)**
2616 Nicollet Ave.
Minneapolis, MN 55408
612-871-7878
contact@aafs.net
www.aafs.net

**American Psychological
Association**
750 First Street, NE
Washington, DC 20002-4242
800-374-2721 or 202-336-5500
www.apa.org

**American Association of Marriage
and Family Therapy**
112 South Alfred Street
Alexandria, VA 22314-3061
703-838-9808
www.aamft.org

American Self-Help Clearinghouse
Northwest Covenant Medical
Center
25 Pocono Rd.
Denville, NJ 07834-2995
973-625-3037
http://mentalhelp.net/selfhelp

AVANCE Family Support and Education Program, Inc.
National Headquarters
118 North Medina
San Antonio, TX 78207
210-270-4630
www.avance.org

Association for Conflict Resolution
1015 18th Street NW, Suite 1150
Washington, DC 20036
202-464-9700
www.acrnet.org

Big Brother Big Sisters of America (BBBSA)
230 N. 13th Street
Philadelphia, PA 19107
215-567-7000
www.bbbsa.org

Center for Child Protection and Family Support
714 G St., SE
Washington, DC 20003
202-544-3144
www.centerchildprotection.org

Children's Rights Council
6200 Editors Park Drive
Hyattsville, MD 20782
301-559-3120
www.gocrc.com

Coalition for Asian American Children and Families
50 Broad St., Suite 1701
New York, NY 10004
212-785-4601
www.cacf.org

Committee for Hispanic Children and Families, Inc. (CHCF)
140 W. 22nd St.
Suite 301
New York, NY 10011
212-206-1090
www.chcfinc.org

Family Support America (formerly Family Resource Coalition of America)
205 W Randolph St., Suite 2222
Chicago, IL 60606
312-338-0900
www.familysupportamerica.org

MELD: Programs to Strengthen Families (MELD)
219 North 2nd St., Suite 200
Minneapolis, MN 55401
612-332-7563
www.meld.org

National Center for Missing and Exploited Children (NCMEC)
Charles B. Wang International
Children's Building
699 Prince St.
Alexandria, VA 22314-3175
800-THE-LOST
(800-843-5678)
www.missingkids.com

National Child Care Information Center (NCCIC)
243 Church St., NW
2nd Floor
Vienna, VA 22180
800-616-2242
www.nccic.org

National Clearinghouse for Alcohol and Drug Information (NCADI)
11420 Rockville Pike
Rockville, MD 20852
800-729-6686
www.health.org

National Clearinghouse on Child Abuse and Neglect Information
330 C Street, S.W.
Washington, DC 20447
800-FYI-3366
http://nccanch.acf.hhs.gov

National Clearinghouse on
Families & Youth (NCFY)
P.O. Box 13505
Silver Spring, MD 20911-3505
301-608-8098
www.ncfy.com

National Congress of
American Indians (NCAI)
1301 Connecticut Ave. NW,
Suite 200
Washington, DC 20036
202-466-7767
www.ncai.org

National Congress for
Fathers and Children
9454 W. Wilshire Blvd.
Suite 907
Beverly Hills, CA 90212
800-733-3237
http://ncfc.net/ncfc

National Indian Child Welfare
Association (NICWA)
5100 SW Macadam Ave., Suite
300
Portland, OR 97239
503-222-4044
www.nicwa.org

National Information Center for
Children and Youth with
Disabilities (NICHCY)
PO Box 1492
Washington, DC 20013
800 695-0285
www.nichcy.org

National Maternal and Child
Health Clearinghouse (NMCHC)
888-ASK-HRSA
(888-275-4772)
www.ask.hrsa.gov/MCH.cfm

National Self-Help Clearinghouse
Graduate School and University
Center of the City University of
New York
365 5th Ave., Suite 3300
New York, NY 10016
212-817-1822
www.selfhelpweb.org

Parents Anonymous
675 West Foothill Blvd.
Suite 220
Claremont, CA 91711-3475
909-621-6184
www.parentsanonymous.org

Parents without Partners
1650 South Dixie Highway, Suite
510
Boca Raton, FL 33432
561-391-8833
www.parentswithoutpartners.org

Single and Custodial Father's
Network, Inc.
608 Hastings Street
Pittsburgh, PA 15206
412-853-9903
www.scfn.org

Single Parents Association
4727 E. Bell Road, Suite 45
PMB 209
Phoenix, AZ 85032
623-581-7445
www.singleparents.org

Stepfamily Foundation
333 West End Ave.
New York, NY 10023
212-877-3244
www.stepfamily.org

Stepfamily Association of America
650 J Street, Suite 205
Lincoln, NE 68508
800-735-0329
www.saafamilies.org

Supervised Visitation Network
2804 Paran Pointe Drive
Cookeville, TN 38506
931-537-3414
www.svnetwork.net

**Zero to Three: National Center
for Infants, Toddlers and Families**
2000 M Street NW, Suite 200
Washington, DC 20036
202-638-1144
www.zerotothree.org

HOTLINES FOR PARENTS

Missing/Abducted Children
Child Find of America
800-I-AM-LOST
(800-426-5678)

Child Find of America Mediation
800-A-WAY-OUT
(800-292-9688)

**Child Quest International
Sighting Line**
888-818-HOPE
(888-818-4673)

**National Center for Missing
and Exploited Children**
800-THE-LOST
(800-843-5678)

**Operation Lookout National
Center for Missing Youth**
800-LOOKOUT
(800-566-5688)

Family Violence
**Family Violence National
Domestic Violence Hotline**
800-799-SAFE
(800-799-7233)

BOOKS FOR CHILDREN

It's Not Your Fault Koko Bear
by Vicki Lansky

Let's Talk About It: Divorce
by Fred Rogers

Two Homes by Claire Masurel

Mama and Daddy Bear's Divorce
by Cornelia Maude

Why Are We Getting a Divorce?
by Peter Mayle

*The Divorce Workbook:
A Guide for Kids and Families*
Ives, Fassler and Lash

*Now I have a Stepparent and It's
Kind of Confusing*
by Janice S. Stenson

*My Parents Still Love Me Even
Though They're Getting Divorced*
by Lois V. Nightingale

*Let's Talk About Living in a
Blended Family*
by Elizabeth Weitzman

*Families are Forever!
Kids Workbook for Sharing
Feelings About Divorce*
by Melissa F. Smith

*Don't Fall Apart on Saturdays!
The Children's Divorce Survival
Book*
by Adolph Moser and David
Melton

*Divorce Happens to the Nicest
Kids: A Self-Help Book for Kids*
by Michael S. Prokop

Divorced, But Still My Parents
by Thomas Shirley

The Suitcase Kid
by Jacqueline Wilson

At Daddy's on Saturday
by Linda Walvoord Girard

The Boy's and Girl's Book about Divorce, with an Introduction for Parents
by Richard Gardner

Can Anyone Fix My Broken Heart? Hope for Children of Divorce
by June Thomas Crews

Dear Daddy by John Schindel

Divorce (Preteen Pressures)
by Debra Goldentyer

Divorce: Young People Caught in the Middle
by Beth Levin

For Better, For Worse: A Guide to Surviving Divorce for Preteens and Their Families
by Janet Bode

Goodbye Daddy
by Brigitte Weninger

How It Feels When Parents Divorce
by Jill Krementz

WEBSITES AND ORGANIZATIONS FOR CHILDREN

Banana Splits
(children's divorce support group)
53 Columbus Avenue #2
New York, NY 10023
212-262-4562

It's Not Your Fault
www.itsnotyourfault.org

BOOKS FOR TEENS

Caught in the Middle: A Teen Guide to Custody
by Claudia Isler

Finding Your Place: A Teen Guide to Life in a Blended Family
by Julie Leibowitz

Help! A Girl's Guide to Divorce and Stepfamilies
from American Girl

It's Not the End of the World
by Judy Blume

Keeping Your Life Together When Your Parents Pull Apart: A Teen's Guide to Divorce
by Angela Elwell Hunt

Money Matters: A Teen Guide to the Economics of Divorce
by Carlienne Frisch

No Easy Answers: A Teen Guide to Why Divorce Happens
by Florence Calhoun

Teens with Single Parents: Why Me?
by Margaret A. Schultz

Understanding the Law: A Teen Guide to Family Court and Minor's Rights
by Anne Bianchi

Why Me? A Teen Guide to Divorce and Your Feelings
by Rachel Aydt

Appendix C

CANADIAN RESOURCES

NOTE: *The resources in this section are specifically for those who are parenting in Canada. If you are in Canada, you should use these resources, but you should also check Appendix B. Most of the books and websites in that appendix are useful for all parents.*

BOOKS FOR PARENTS

Canadian Parents Sourcebook
by Roseman, Darragh

Complete Book of Mother and Baby Care
by Canadian Medical Association

BOOKS FOR CHILDREN

Surviving Your Parents' Divorce: A Guide for Young Canadians
by Michael Cochrane

WEBSITES AND ORGANIZATIONS

Big Brothers and Big Sisters of Canada
3228 South Service Road,
Suite 113E
Burlington, Ontario
L7N 3H8
800-263-9133
www.bigsisters.ca

The Canadian Association for Young Children
www.cayc.ca/index2.html

Canadian Association of Family Resource Programs
707 - 331 Cooper Street
Ottawa ON   K2P 0G5
613-237-7667
www.frp.ca

Canadian Council for Co-Parenting
613-223-0273

Canadian Mental Health Association
8 East King Street, Suite 810
Toronto, ON M5C 1B5
416-484-7750
www.cmha.ca

Canadian Parents
www.canadianparents.com

Canadian Parents Online
www.canadianparents.com

Child CyberSearch Missing Children Database and Information
www.childcybersearch.org

Department of Justice (Canada)
http://canada.justice.gc.ca

Divorce and Defence Strategies (Canada)
416-243-9582
www.dadscanada.com

Equal Parents of Canada Mailing List
www.interlog.com/%7Eparental/
   epocnews/home.htm

Equitable Child Maintenance and Access Society (Canada)
780-988-4015
www.geocities.com/CapitolHill/
   Lobby/2302

Family Service Canada
404-383 Parkdale Avenue
Ottawa, ON
K1Y 4R4
800-668-7808
www.familyservicecanada.org

Human Equality Action and Resource Team (HEART-Canada)
2 A The Marketplace
East York, ON
M4C 5M1
416-698-3655
www.interlog.com/~parental

Kids Help (Canada): Help for Children of Divorce
800-668-6868
http://kidshelp.sympatico.ca

Legal Information for Canada
http://library.lsuc.on.ca/GL/
   home.htm

Men's and Father's Support Groups Across Canada
www.canlaw.com/rights/fathers.htm

Men's Education Support Association (Canada)
Box 4691 Stn C
Calgary, Alberta
T2T 5P1
www.mesacanada.com

North America Missing Children Association
www.namca.com

One Parent Families Association of Canada
1099 Kingston Rd. Suite 222
Pickering, ON
L1V 1B5
905-831-7098
www.oneparentfamilies
   association.ca

Ontario StepFamily Association
www.angelfire.com/on3/onstep

Parent and Child Advocacy Coalition (Canada)
http://pcaccanada.tripod.com

Parent Help Line (Canada)
888-603-9100

Parents without Partners
international number
561-391-3833

Rainbows
17 Theresa Street
Barrie, ON L4M 1J5
877-403-2733
www.rainbows.org
An organization that provides peer support groups for children of all ages and adults who are or have experienced divorce.

Single Parents World (Canada)
www.parentsworld.com

Supervised Visitation in Ontario: information and resources
www.attorneygeneral.jus.gov.on.ca/
   english/family/supaccess.asp

To Report Child Abuse in Canada:

Kids Help Hotline
800-668-6868

Appendix D

TELEPHONE NUMBERS FOR REPORTING CHILD ABUSE (STATE BY STATE)

For states not listed, or when the reporting party resides in a different state than the child, call **Childhelp, 800-4-A-Child** (800-422-4453), or your local CPS agency.

Alabama (AL)
334-242-9500
(report by county)

Alaska (AK)
800-478-4444

Arizona (AZ)
888-SOS-CHILD
(888-767-2445)

Arkansas (AR)
800-482-5964

Connecticut (CT)
800-842-2288
800-624-5518
(TDD/hearing impaired)

Delaware (DE)
800-292-9582

District of Columbia
887-671-SAFE

Florida (FL)
800-96-ABUSE
(800-962-2873)

Illinois (IL)
800-252-2873

Indiana (IN)
800-562-2407

Iowa (IA)
800-362-2178

Kansas (KS)
800-922-5330

Kentucky (KY)
800-752-6200

Maine (ME)
800-452-1999

Maryland (MD)
800-332-6347

Massachusetts (MA)
800-792-5200

Michigan (MI)
800-942-4357

Mississippi (MS)
800-222-8000

Missouri (MO)
800-392-3738

Montana (MT)
800-332-6100

Nebraska (NE)
800-652-1999

Nevada (NV)
800-992-5757

New Hampshire (NH)
800-894-5533

New Jersey (NJ)
800-792-8610
800-835-5510
(TDD/hearing impaired)

New Mexico (NM)
800-797-3260

New York (NY)
800-342-3720

North Carolina (NC)
800-662-7030

North Dakota (ND)
800-245-3736

Oklahoma (OK)
800-522-3511

Oregon (OR)
800-854-3508

Pennsylvania (PA)
800-932-0313

Rhode Island (RI)
800-RI-CHILD
(800-742-4453)

Texas (TX)
800-252-5400

Utah (UT)
800-768-9399

Virginia (VA)
800-552-7096

Washington (WA)
800-562-5624

West Virginia (WV)
800-352-6513

Wyoming (WY)
800-457-3659

Index

visitation, 1, 2, 3, 6, 7, 8, 15,
21, 22, 48, 49, 51, 53, 57,
58, 61, 63, 67, 73, 76, 61-
77, 80, 81, 83, 84, 85, 86,
94, 97-102, 103-111, 113,
114, 117, 129, 131, 133
child refuses to go, 87, 88
coping with, 61
long distance, 97-102, 133
others involved with, 103
plan, 45
schedule, 14, 53, 55, 127
skipping, 48, 82, 120, 133
supervised, 128-129

W

weekends, 56, 61, 113
withdrawal, 12
working out problems, 82

ABOUT THE AUTHOR

Brette McWhorter Sember is a retired divorce and family attorney and family mediator. She focused her practice on representing children in divorce and custody cases. She was on the Law Guardian panel in three different New York state counties As part of this role, she visited child clients in their homes, visited their schools, saw them interact with both parents, and facilitated and attended therapy sessions with them when needed. She worked closely with parents, teachers, social workers, and therapists, as well as attorneys for both sides.

Sember is the author of sixteen books, including *File for Divorce in New York*; *Child Custody, Visitation and Support in New York*; *The Divorce Organizer and Planner*, and *No-Fight Divorce*.

Her website is **www.BretteSember.com**.